Seriously, It's Just High School Football

By: Larry Kovac

PublishAmerica
Baltimore

© 2006 by Larry Kovac.
All rights reserved. No part of this book may be reproduced, stored in a retrieval system or transmitted in any form or by any means without the prior written permission of the publishers, except by a reviewer who may quote brief passages in a review to be printed in a newspaper, magazine or journal.

First printing

ISBN: 1-4137-9931-0
PUBLISHED BY PUBLISHAMERICA, LLLP
www.publishamerica.com
Baltimore

Printed in the United States of America

Dedicated to those great police officers whom I have had the pleasure of knowing very well as co-workers, friends and family, who have gone on before me, and although their loss to me on this Earth leaves a hole in my heart, I know full well that Heaven is a lot safer place after their arrival there.

Patrolman Andrew Kovac
Youngstown, Ohio Police Department

Patrolman Ralph DeSalle
Youngstown, Ohio Police Department

Sgt. Francis Malone
Youngstown, Ohio Police Department

Detective Vic Cioffredi
New York City Police Department

Detective Richie "Poppy" Sanchez
New York City Police Department

TABLE OF CONTENTS

INTRODUCTION 7

CHAPTER I: SOME THINGS YOU JUST CAN'T TEACH 9
CHAPTER II: THE CHARACTERS 16
CHAPTER III: GETTING STARTED 30
CHAPTER IV: GETTING THERE 46
CHAPTER V: WE'RE HERE! 56
CHAPTER VI: TAKING THE FIELD 71
CHAPTER VII: LET'S GET THE SHOW ON THE ROAD 91
CHAPTER VIII: HALFTIME! 112
CHAPTER IX: ARE WE DONE YET? 121
CHAPTER X: THE GAME IS OVER 140
CHAPTER XI: 9/11 155
CHAPTER XII: WRAPPING THINGS UP 159

APPLE AND SAUSAGE STUFFING (DOUBLE BATCH) 177
MISTER SHY'S SAUCE 178

INTRODUCTION

I have a story to tell. Is it something that people will want to read because it will move them and change their lives? I think not. So what am I trying to say and why?

I have read several books by distinguished NFL referees and a couple of coaches. The works seem to tell of their rise from a humble beginning to the pinnacle of their profession and the trials and sacrifices made along the way. They are the few of the thousands of men and women who have gotten into the arena of high school sports officiating for whatever reason and have managed to rise through the ranks to the top of their chosen sport.

Me, I have not risen to the pinnacle of anything, at least by my take on it. All I have managed to do is go out there every Friday and a few Saturdays for ten to twelve weeks out of the year and officiate high school football games for over twenty years.

In the process I have had a heck of a lot of fun and along the way have made a few good friends.

One day I came to the realization that maybe I'm not a big time college or pro football official, but nonetheless the games I worked are important to those who are involved. I also came to appreciate the fact that I was one of thousands of football officials who go out on those same Fridays and Saturdays just as I did. They, as me, did not rise to become big time college or pro football officials but without them a lot of people would not get to enjoy high school football.

This work is a tribute to those thousands of high school football officials who, like myself, put in long hours for little pay but the rewards are much more than any game fees may be.

My story then is aimed at those who might identify with a situation or condition that I have experienced and have a good laugh.

To the people who are not sports officials, maybe they will see a side of high school sports that they did not see before.

CHAPTER I

SOME THINGS YOU JUST CAN'T TEACH

I have spent my football officiating career in the state of Arizona, but I was born and raised in northeast Ohio where high school football is immensely popular. In some small towns the following of the local high school football team is like a religion to those people and the towns literally grind to a halt on Fridays in the fall. I used to say if a town had 2,000 residents there would be 1,978 of them in the stands on a Friday night with the other twenty-two down on the field. Prior to moving to Arizona I lived in a one such small town of McDonald, Ohio, located a few miles northwest of Youngstown, Ohio, just next to Girard. Like the other cities in the area the local economy relied on the steel industry, which had taken a turn for the worse in the late 1970s. Despite the depressing news of the local steel company's departure, it did little to dampen the spirits of the fans who would be shoe-horned into every space possible in their small stadium to watch those home games on Friday nights. They would shoot off fireworks to announce the start of the games and again when the home team would score, which was often, considering they had and still have one of the better programs of any small school in the area.

You can imagine my surprise when I was assigned on of my first high school games in the state of Arizona, which was the first home game of the year for the reigning state champions Trevor Browne on the west side of Phoenix. I could only think what it would be like doing the home opener of an Ohio state football champion such as Massilon or Canton McKinley and the huge crowd that it would attract. I envisioned a high school football stadium that was overflowing with a huge, enthusiastic crowd. Well, you can imagine my disappointment when we took the field a half hour before the game and I was very surprised to see that there were less than a thousand people there. When the game started the stands were only half full if that much.

My first exposure to high school sports, football in particular began in the late 1950s and early 1960s when I was growing up in Youngstown, Ohio. My brother Gib was playing football for our high school Woodrow Wilson High. My father would try to take me to see each game, and since he was a policeman he would have to work on a few of the nights there were games, so he would see to it that I would get to the games with one of our neighbors whose sons played on the team, also.

High school football is hugely popular in northeast Ohio and still is to this day and that was evident with our neighbors whom we would see at the games or who would take me in the absence of my dad. Mr. McCabe or Mr. Lavalglio, whose sons were teammates of my brother, would load me into one of their cars and we would head off to Rayen or South High Stadium to see the games since there were eight high schools and only two football fields at that time. It was on those Friday nights, much to my mother's chagrin that I would learn the four-letter expletives that dot my conversations to this day. I should note that on those Friday nights the exploits of the Woodrow Wilson High School football team resulted more often than not in defeat, so the naughty adjectives used to fly frequently.

I must admit that despite the losses, each Friday meant as much to me as it did to the more successful programs. Even recently when I was contacting some of the people (whose real names I have used) to get their permission to do so, I had the opportunity to speak with our former neighbor Dennis McCabe. We were talking about our old high school and its lack of success, and he said, "You have to really love football to play for Wilson."

Despite the lack of success the games were an opportunity to watch my brother and our neighbors go out and try to win each night, and we didn't realize at the time that it afforded a real opportunity to see something that would not be there forever, my brother or say Paul Krispinsky or Dennis McCabe playing football, something they have not done for close to forty years.

Those nine or ten Friday and Saturday nights each year were something special to me growing up. With the end of the school week drawing near, the anticipation of that week's high school game was the focal point of each conversation among my other male classmates. Usually, our anxiety would begin to rise as the junior high or junior varsity team would play right after school and my friends and I would attend the games and see kids who we had just gone to grade school with but were a year or two older in those games.

The games would wrap up just about the time that football practice would be wrapping up so we would see the "big boys" from the varsity team leaving the practice field adjacent to the field where the freshman games were played. I would look for my brother leaving the field along with his teammates who were also our neighbors. I'd usually try to get their attention and say, "Hi!" When Paul Krispinsky, Ron Demesko or our next door neighbor Denny McCabe would acknowledge me, I would be smiling with delight, kind of like, *Hey, I know those guys!* I would be looking around for my classmates who might be exiting the freshman game with me like I was some kind of big shot. By the time Friday night (and a few Saturdays) rolled around the kids in the neighborhood and I would really be revved up in anticipation of the big game. It would not matter that the records of both teams might not be the best; to us it was the only game that mattered. It was the recollection of that anticipation that would benefit me later in my officiating career to realize that the game you're doing that night is just as important to those kids on that day as those games were to me so many years ago.

On the night of the game I would leave to go to the games with my dad or whichever neighbor was driving us to the game. There would be the enthusiasm as we approached the site of the game and it heightened considerably once the sights, sounds and smells tantalized our youthful senses.

The sights began as we approached Rayen or South High Stadium with the glow of the lights of the stadium guiding us, like a beacon to an approaching aircraft. The glorious colors of the trees dressed in all their autumn colors, the explosive reds, yellows and oranges of the season. Of course, there was the unmistakable nip in the air created by the brisk chill that accompanies the arrival of the fall season. Depending on the time of our arrival we might catch sight of the large buses arriving with the football teams or each school's respective band.

The sounds of the vendors yelling "Programs, get your programs!" greeted me as I entered the stadium, and once inside the vendors were selling everything from popcorn to candied apples (unlike in Arizona where you could purchase such oh-so-traditional football snacks like *nachos*). One would hear the brisk "One, two three, four!" cadence as the teams did their calisthenics, warming up before the game with the occasional chirp of a coach's whistle summoning a group of players together for the next set of warm-ups.

Of course no night would be complete without the spirited pounding of drums as the marching bands would make their way from the buses to the sidelines and eventually the field for the pre-game festivities.

The smells one associates with a Friday night football game cannot be mistaken. The burning of pipe or cigar tobacco mixed with the crisp odor of burning leaves. The stadium concession stands with burgers and hot dogs grilling, coffee brewing along with pizza and popcorn being kept warm. If you were lucky enough to get close to the high school cheerleaders you got an ample whiff of their perfume, quite a thrill for a fourth or fifth grader like I was at the time.

SERIOUSLY, IT'S JUST HIGH SCHOOL FOOTBALL

I know now that there were probably hundreds of high school football games being played on those nights but regardless of their record, none were more important than the one I was attending on that evening. In another part of the state of Ohio, Massillon may be squaring off against Canton McKinley, two perennial powerhouses, but wild horses could not have pulled me away from Woodrow Wilson against say for example, Chaney, a City Series rival on this night.

It is because of this experience that I hold closely the viewpoint a veteran official shared with me early in my officiating career.

He told me that no matter how insignificant the game may be in the overall scheme of things (playoff implications, rivalry, etc.), treat each game with the same degree of respect that the kids have of it. Even though it does not have much of a bearing on the final standings, to those kids, coaches and those in attendance, (just as it was to me all those years ago) that game is just as important to them as the Super Bowl, and to keep it in mind. Just as my own, my brother's, and his teammates' football careers are long over, that same veteran told me, "You may be back out to officiate a game here at that same school again next year for a football game, but to most of the kids, they will not!" I knew he was right as I look back on the games of my brother and during my brief but ineffective career. There were a lot of guys that I knew who once their high school years were over never played organized ball again.

My objective has always been not to take myself, as an official, too seriously or to over-emphasize my importance. I have worked games with guys that have contests prior to the games to see who could throw their penalty flags the furthest. One other guy showed up with a penalty flag in each pocket of his knickers (four in all) in case he had multiple fouls on a single play. That is not my idea of being a football official. It is after all high school football and I think our goal is to teach as well as keep order.

There was another guy who fell into the taking-himself-too-seriously category. He envisioned being a referee and having his own crew some day, so much so that he would wear a white referee's crew chief's hat to work Pop Warner games on Saturday mornings when all other officials wore black hats with the white striping.

I think it is a good idea to go out and have fun and make the game run as smoothly as possible and do so humbly. Not as one official I knew who used to like to brag about his accomplishments to the point of being annoying.

The ultimate came one year just as the season was winding down. I usually have a Christmas party for my friends and it coincides with the end of the season and this one year this guy shows up and he had just done a playoff game and ends up at my party. Our entire crew was there and we had not gotten a playoff game, which we never let get us down until this one evening. This guy is in my kitchen and pointing to his shoes and saying, "Take a look at this, fellows; what you see on the bottom of those shoes is playoff-game mud!" Like I said there are guys who take themselves too seriously. But, this fellow really broke my bananas. I told myself I would never elevate myself to such a pinnacle of self-importance and if I did, to please give me a well-deserved kick in the ass.

I spent a great deal of my life in law enforcement and as a full-time and volunteer officer with three agencies, and anyone will tell you that you are going to be more successful talking to people rather than throwing everyone in jail. In the long run being pro-active has its advantages. That in mind, having spent most of my working days in a stressful environment, the last thing I needed was to create one in my hobbies, i.e. football.

I found that talking to the kids during a game is a good way to get a feel for what's happening and in the meantime establishing a rapport with them just as I have so many times on the streets. But, I mean this in a good way, when you have the kids feel that you are an authority figure but still not an adversary, the results are unique to say the least. This is especially true the younger the player.

One Saturday I was doing a flag football game in Pop Warner and those kids are only about six or seven years old. The guys that coach at this level deserve a medal for their patience because it takes a real concerted effort to round up the eight players before each play and keep them on one side of the football to line up. Forget about complex plays, if they can get the kids to line up, stay still long enough to hike the ball without jumping offside and do so in the forty-five-second allotted interval between plays (more like a minute and a half), it is a miracle. As an official at this level I am more a helper in this chaos than an official, having to retrieve one little tyke after another and escort them to their team huddle, sideline or for the most part just their side of the ball.

One little guy seemed to have a shorter attention span than all the others and was continuously being mesmerized by aircraft flying overhead as we were in the glide path to Sky Harbor Airport. I had to continuously usher the little tyke back to his side of the ball after each play because his focus was skyward as one jumbo jet after another circled overhead and he would just stand there in the middle of the field in a trance-like gaze at a jumbo jet so close you almost felt you could toss a rock and hit it. I would have to go over to him on more that one occasion, tap him on the shoulder and say, "Come on, little guy, let's get you back on your side of the ball." He would just shrug and wander back to his teammates at least until the next scheduled arrival at Sky Harbor. When the game was over I felt a tug at my leg and the little guy was draped around my leg hanging on for dear life like I was a long lost relative. The little kid looked up at me with the biggest grin and huge enthusiastic brown eyes and asked, "Who won?"

That little kid seemed to sum it all up for me. He was the ultimate example of what the game is supposed to be about, having fun. He was kind of playing football, all the while checking out the airplanes and befriending this huge goofy-looking guy wearing this striped shirt who was nice enough to assure it he made it back to his team's huddle in a timely fashion and just having a grand old time. In the end all he was concerned about was the Dairy Queen or Chuck E. Cheese's or whatever fast food he was about to enjoy once his game was completed, the outcome of the game the furthest thing from his mind.

I hope the little kid grows up to be a football official. If not, the President of the United States. It is to him and thousands of other football officials that this book is dedicated.

CHAPTER II

THE CHARACTERS

I guess you could say that I haven't taken myself serious from an early age. When I was a little tyke about three or four years old, my mother would be talking on the telephone and I used to think it was a neat trick to run out the back door of our house which sat on the corner of Gibson and Cambridge in Youngstown, Ohio. I would run around to the front and ring the front door bell. My mother who had been on the phone would put the phone down thinking someone was at the front door, having totally forgotten about me. She would open the front door looking for a visitor and there I would be laughing my head off. She would drag me back into the house and scold me. Although I do not remember it, my brother Gib tells me that the most memorable of these stunts occurred on a Saturday afternoon during the summer.

My mother had given me a bath and was drying me off when the phone rang. She answered the phone and while talking I bolted out the back door butt naked and was running around the house toward the front door as I have done in the past. Apparently, a motorist traveling up Gibson Street was laughing so hard he drove up over the curb and almost clipped the fire hydrant in front of our house.

SERIOUSLY, IT'S JUST HIGH SCHOOL FOOTBALL

I truly believe that you can go out and do a job or complete a task without drawing a lot of attention to yourself or over-emphasizing your own importance. Again, I developed that attitude with respect to sports early in life. It was obvious that I was going to be a big boy having topped out at 6'3" and tipping the scale at a dainty 240 pounds. My brother Gib is even bigger than I am at 6'5", and our parents taught us that you earn respect from others by being an honest and decent individual rather than trying to demand it through intimidation and bullying. In fact all you get using the latter is fear, not respect.

When I was in Woodrow Wilson High School in Youngstown in the 1960s, I didn't play a lot of varsity football or any other sports for that matter probably because I wasn't any good at it. That isn't to say that I didn't enjoy playing sports even if it was a pick-up game, whether it was in a neighbor's back yard or on a local playground. That was because it was fun. What little Spanish I have learned, I think sports is referred to as "*deportes*." This was easy because "*deportes*" is similar to "departure" which is how I have viewed sports, as a departure from schoolwork, household chores or after-school jobs.

It was in those high school years when I encountered two or three guys in my graduating class of 1969 who took themselves way too seriously. They just the type of bullying, intimidating horse's asses who delighted in pushing teammates down in the mud, poking them in the arm with pencils or pummeling them with tackling dummies. But much to their credit, when you play on a high school football team that collectively over three years is a combined 3-21-1, you have to prove how tough you are by shoving around your slower, weaker teammates since you sure as hell aren't proving it a lot on Friday nights against your opponents. There were times I wondered if I could purposely flunk a course or two and return with the junior class who were most of my circle of friends and had a better chance of gridiron success, but eventually I came to my senses and completed the senior year, and went on about life.

A magnificent example of a guy who enjoyed a sport and didn't take it too seriously is a fellow we called Gene "The Chicken Man."

My brother Gib and I played golf with a local radio celebrity who asked us if we wanted to play on his radio station's benefit basketball team. We would go to local high schools and play against their faculty for charity. We would not get a cent for these games but did raise money for some worthy causes and it was quite rewarding. In playing these games most of the faculty members are ex-jocks and view these contests as a means to resurrect a long lost athletic career and the games take on an importance of the NCAA Final Four. To say that some of these faculty members are intense is an understatement.

Now Gene wasn't very tall, was on the portly side, didn't move too fast and wasn't what you would call a natural athlete. That didn't stop him from having a generous personality and he just thoroughly enjoyed participating in the games. Gene would get into games when the score was lopsided which was just about every night. When Gene would take the court he would usually take up a position somewhere in the vicinity of the opposition's basket partly because Gene didn't move real well and partly by design.

It wouldn't take long before one of the ex-jocks would steal an errant pass or dribble and take off down court. There would be short, chubby, slow moving Gene standing between him and an uncontested slam dunk that, had there been ESPN in the early 1970s, would unquestionably have made the highlight reel. Only, at the precise moment, usually at the apex of the Michael Jordan wannabe's leap, Gene would reach under his sweat shirt and produce a rubber chicken that he would gently toss into the face of the rim-bound opponent. This would startle the living daylights out of him, throwing his timing completely off. One guy's attempt at a slam dunk ricocheted off the back of the rim, soaring clean out near mid-court.

This would result in a chorus of hoots and jeers directed at the faculty member, and the more unpopular the offending teacher was with the student body the louder the hoots and jeers. After we got accustomed to Gene's M.O. we would pick out the biggest hot dog on the opposition. We would just about deliberately toss the ball to him and dog it on defense to further enhance his fast break opportunity just to be able to enjoy Gene's antics.

I think in a previous life Gene "The Chicken Man" was a Harlem Globetrotter.

Another guy I know also helped in creating my "don't-take-this-stuff-too-seriously" attitude is Tom "The Hawk" Benton. Tom and I met when I was a senior in high school when we played for several years on a fast pitch softball team, which was mediocre at best, but not without its share of characters. Like for example we had a pitcher who wore a cowboy hat, which is quite uncommon is northeast Ohio, as the league's uniform requirements were somewhat lax. I was the catcher and this kid had a rocket for an arm, but his control was erratic, especially to left-handed batters. In fact, one night he hit the same left-handed batsman four times in successive at bats.

Tom had the quickest hands and feet of any athlete I ever laid eyes on which was evidenced by the fact that he lettered in tennis for Youngstown State University. As big as his talent were his sense of humor and flair for the mischievous. Tom played shortstop or second base and over the years had to field more than one of my throws to second base that from time to time had a tendency to sail into center field. As spotty as the pitcher's control was to the plate were some of my throws to second base, the result of which were frequent walks and numerous base runners. It didn't take long for word to spread about my equally erratic throws to second base, so base-stealing attempts were numerous.

Our league played in an inner city park called Volney Rogers where they did not leave anything lying around because of the high theft rate in the adjoining neighborhood. When you arrived for the scheduled game, there was a guard shack at the bottom of the hill where you had to sign out the bases and once the game was over you had to return them. There were no pegs in the ground to tie the bases down, just wooden stakes pounded into the ground so you knew where to put them down.

One game we were playing the undefeated first place team and the pitcher had alarmingly accurate control this night, and it was one of those nights when we "caught lighting in a bottle," as they say, and were playing a nearly flawless game, winning in the late innings. The first batter, a portly left-handed batter, walked and was bunted over to second base with the next batter legging out a single, putting runners at first and third with one out and it looked like once again we were going to blow the lead. The runner on first was a guy who had a slight speech impediment that worsened if he was excited. The next batter was up at the plate and right off the bat, sure as hell, the runner on first base breaks for second base in yet another attempted steal. When I catch the pitch at home plate I let loose a throw to second base that looked okay when it left my hand but began to sail. Tom went to cover the bag.

Now, let me say this, I learned later in life that cops who are in shootouts have said that it appears that they happen in slow motion and fortunately, I have never been in one so I'll have to take them at their words because what happened next seemed to me to be in slow motion because I can still recall it to this day. Tom began to leap upward to try to snare my errant throw and it looked like even if the ball didn't soar into center field, by the time he would come down the runner would beat the throw. But, in pure Little Rascals style, Tom's foot gave the base the slightest nudge, enough to cause it to move about six to eight inches toward left field. Tom snatched the ball out of the air at the apex of his leap and came down to make the tag on the runner who would have normally been safe but his slide came up about a half a foot short.

The umpire who bore a striking resemblance to the actor Pat Paulsen of *Rowan and Martin's Laugh-In* fame called the runner out. At that point he gets up pointing frantically to the base, but his speech impediment kicked in big time and all he could sputter was, "He k-k-k-k-kicked the b-b-b-b-b-b…" when the umpire yelled an even more emphatic, "Yerr OUT!!!"

The runner continued his complaint, "B-b-b-b-but he k-k-k-k…" and the ump yelled, "You're out, one more word out of you and you're gone!" Meanwhile, Tom tossed the ball to me to assure the runner did not score from third while the downtrodden base runner continued back to their bench muttering all the way. We went on to win the game, pinning the only loss of the season on our opponent by the narrowest of margins.

On another occasion we were playing a team that was clearly better than us and the score showed, but the opposition that day had a reputation of being a bunch of crybabies and this day had no reason to bitch because they were really socking it to us. As big a bunch of whiners as they were, the biggest were their first baseman and pitcher, one of whom was of all things a college professor. In our half of the inning we were at bat and Tom was batting and I was in the on-deck circle. Tom hit a slow dribbler up the third base line that the third baseman had a devil of a time with and when he made his throw to first base, the ball and Tom, the runner arrived at precisely the same time in what would be called a classic "bang-bang" play. The umpire called Tom safe and the first baseman immediately slammed the ball to the ground and began screaming, "You have to be out of your goddamn mind!" and charged one of the two umpires working the game.

As soon as he did that, the pitcher stormed off the mound and headed toward first base as did most of their infield. Of course while this was going on I guess nobody on the opposing team realized that since time was not called that technically the ball was still in play although both the umpires had their hands full with the full-scale argument going on. I was thinking, *Gee, this would be a good time for Tom to take an extra base*, and evidently he had the same thought, because he took an extra base in the confusion, *third base!* I stood in the on deck circle and watched in amazement as Tom proceeded to stroll across the diamond amidst, as my brother used to call player/umpire beefs, "a rhubarb," over the pitcher's rubber and calmly onto third base, totally by-passing second base entirely. After a few minutes, order was restored and there was Tom standing on third base like nothing was wrong, but I was hardly able to take my turn at bat as I was laughing so hard. Baseball, or softball as it was in this case, is a game and is supposed to be fun, isn't it?

Since I am naming names, let me tell you about a few individuals who have contributed to this whole production, not to mention to various degrees my outlook on officiating.

Roger Vanderploeg has been a football official and crew chief for over twenty years and has spent just as long as a good friend. Roger, a graduate of the University of Michigan who played football there in the late 1950s, was not always the crew chief. Originally he was one of the sideline officials (linesman, line judge) and our crew chief was a fellow I'll call "Elmer" who was about seventy years old.

Elmer was past his prime and would bitch constantly about the Commissioner of Officials to anyone and everyone whether they wanted to hear about it or not. At that time the economy was pretty slow so there was a glut of people wanting to be sports officials to supplement their income and we were just happy to be on a varsity crew. I am sure that word of Elmer's frequent bitching made its way back to the Commissioner who rewarded him every week by assigning his crew games as far removed from the downtown Phoenix area as humanly possible. Harry Sharrock, the fourth official at the time owned a bar and used to say, "For once I'd like to get back from a game before last call."

After several years of being on the road virtually every week, Roger, Harry and I came to the conclusion that Elmer had to politely be told that his best days were behind him and maybe he should think about hanging it up. I mean something had to be done. I used to joke that when it came time to make our schedule the assignor used to put on a blindfold and take ten darts and throw them at a map of the state of Arizona and those would be the cities we would travel to the following season. The job was left to Roger, so he took Elmer to play tennis one afternoon and after thrashing him soundly got Elmer to reluctantly agree to retire.

After elevating Roger to crew chief, we started getting better games and with his "hey-guys-it's-just-high-school-football" attitude, began having a lot more fun. Add to that the fact that the state map started to shrink and that we were getting home before last call. With the assortment of characters we had assembled I really looked forward to Friday nights, and how many can say that about any job?

The situation with Elmer wasn't the only time we used Roger as the hatchet man. On more than one occasion we had to have him tell an official or two that maybe being a high school football official wasn't for them, or maybe just not our crew. We used to kid him that if Roger asked you to come and play tennis with him you best start shopping around for a new crew. By the way, I don't play tennis; maybe that's why he has kept me around for so long.

Roger is not afraid to say what is on his mind. There was an individual in our association who had a big say-so in our scheduling and had a particular animosity toward Roger and I because we vocally pointed out his prejudices along with the fact that some of the officiating accomplishments he listed on his resume were not only embellished but down right false. The powers that be at the time chose not to do anything when this was brought to light and in fact gave him more power. In 1997 we thought for sure that this situation would lead to us to retire out of frustration, so we decided to do something really special at the end of the season to put the finishing touch on our officiating careers.

Scott Williams is our "do everything" member of our crew in that we can put him out at any position and he will perform just fine. He has pretty much spent most of his life out West and he and Roger came up with the idea of attending a football game in the Midwest or back East someplace. Roger's brother Fred is a season ticket holder at the University of Michigan where he has a block of seats. We came up with an idea to attend the Michigan vs. Ohio State game the weekend before Thanksgiving in 1997.

In Arizona I couldn't get into college football and that was a result of my first visit to an Arizona State game when I first got to the state. A co-worker of mine came up to me one day and asked if I was a football fan and I told him I was. He had two tickets to an ASU home game that he gave me for that Saturday night. I'm sorry but I can't get into a football game where you can see ladies walking up and down the aisle in the grandstands wearing spiked high-heeled shoes and a mink coat in 100-plus degree temperature, so the thought of braving the elements in late November at a college football game was really appealing to me. I figured it would remind me of the good old days in Youngstown, Ohio. Besides, we were not in the Arizona officiating elite at that time so I was sure we would not have a playoff game, which is all there is that time of year.

We made all the arrangements months ahead of time and as the season progressed the OSU/Michigan match-up was looking more and more like it would have a major impact on the Bowl and National Championship picture. By the time the week of the game rolled around tickets to the big game became a very hot item.

The Friday before the game we flew to Detroit and picked up a rental car and checked into our hotel out near the airport in Romulus, Michigan. It was mid-afternoon so we drove up to Ann Arbor as Roger wanted to take us on a tour of the campus. We pulled out of the rental car lot and Scott, who has never experienced a Midwest winter noticed a plastic item clipped to the sun visor and said, "What is this?"

I told him, "You'll find out tomorrow morning because it is supposed to snow tonight and that is a window scraper."

I collect shot glasses and while we were touring the UM campus we stopped into the "M-Den," the team shop on campus to pick one up. Once we were inside the store we saw that there was a news crew from one of the Detroit network stations and this female news reporter was interviewing the store manager. He was telling the news lady that it was something akin to Christmas Eve in the store because of the big game, that people were buying everything off the shelves and they were running out of stock.

The crew had just turned off the camera when Roger, always one to speak his mind just blurts out, "I'll tell you how big this game is, the three of us came all the way from Arizona to see it!"

The female newscaster told the cameraman to turn the camera back on and stuck a microphone in Roger's face and asked him if he had an opinion on what he thought the outcome of the game would be. Without hesitation he said, "There is no question that we (Michigan) are going to win, it is just by how much."

We returned to our hotel and when it got to be around eleven o'clock we turned on the news to see if we might be on TV. Let me tell you how big this game is. In downtown Detroit that evening, an Asian-American store owner was stabbed to death and found on the floor of his business. Even that took a back seat to the big game, and the interview with Roger was the lead story on the broadcast.

The next day we made our way to Michigan Stadium. We got there about one and a half hours before the game. The parking lot adjacent to Crisler Arena was a sight to behold. For as far as one could see there was a solid mass of maize and blue mixed with a thick layer of smoke from all the pre-game grilling that was going on. Scott was amazed at the goings-on there, such as one table that had an ice sculpture of a wolverine in the center of a table fit for a Thanksgiving feast. One bunch of guys who obviously were total strangers and rabid Michigan fans, offered us a beer, and when Scott offered up that I was originally from Ohio, immediately they demanded to know if I was an Ohio State fan. I told him as far as I was concerned there was only one college football team from Ohio that I rooted for and that was the Youngstown State Penguins. With that they let out a hearty "Woof! Woof!" like a Cleveland Browns' Dawg Pound and offered me another beer. We met up with Fred, who had our tickets, and the rest of the Vanderploeg clan. At the game, I don't recall seeing any ladies in mink coats although that day they certainly would have fit in since it was in the thirties with snow flurries. I did meet up with Roger's brother Ken and his wife Sue, who weighs in at maybe a hundred pounds soaking wet and seated directly behind me. So enthusiastic is Sue that she would pound my shoulders every time Michigan made a big play and there were a bunch of them that day. I had so many layers of clothing there was no way she could have hurt me, but I couldn't help but appreciate the enthusiasm. I said to Scott Williams, "Now this is real football."

Buoyed by Roger's eleventh hour prediction, Michigan went on to beat Ohio State and as they say, the rest is history.

Another lifelong friend who just happens to be a football official is Tom Krispinsky. I have known Tom since seventh grade but the history between the Kovac and Krispinsky families goes back even further than that. My brother Gib and Tom's oldest brother Paul are friends also. They played football and graduated from Wilson High School in 1962. I don't know how many mornings I would have frozen my ass off had it not been for Mr. Krispinsky giving me a ride to school, and that was no small task given that I was not as much a stickler for punctuality as I am now that I am older. It was many a cold morning that Tom would call my house to make sure I was up and moving since I had a tendency to sleep in from time to time, to make sure I made to his house before his dad would drive us to school.

Among other things, Tom is the only pitcher I know who has tossed a no hitter in a slow pitch softball game.

Tom has actually made it to what to me is "the big time" since he has become a Big 10 Football official for the last several years. You would never know it. He is still the same great guy he has been for years. While living in Arizona, we kept in touch, and when I came back home to visit we always got together.

Recently, I have retired and moved back to Ohio. I was flying back and was scheduled to land in Pittsburgh. For a while there it looked like I might need a ride from the airport. He offered to pick me up, which would have meant driving over an hour from Youngstown to Pittsburgh despite the fact that he had a school board meeting that night.

In late October of 2003, my mother passed away after a long illness and Tom was the first to call and offer his condolences.

A lot of that goes back I think to our old neighborhood, growing up where you made friends with whole families. As kids there were petty rivalries, but as we grew into teenagers and young adults you learned about loyalties to your neighbors and those relationships stay with you throughout your life. When my brother Gib got married in 1991, I went back to our old South Side neighborhood and just for the heck of it I dropped in on our old next door neighbor the Campanas, whom I hadn't seen in over ten years. They were just as glad to see me as if I had just returned from a two-week vacation. Mr. Campana gave me a beer and Mrs. C. offered to make me dinner.

That goes for sports, too. Tom and I spent hours at the Taft School playground or Shady Run ball field playing whatever sport was in season. As soon as the weather broke, the kids would file out of their houses like a prison jailbreak and there was never any shortage of pick-up football, baseball or basketball games. At the time in Youngstown, Ohio, there were eight high schools that all fielded varsity football teams. There were only two football stadiums and you add to that the fact that one of them was shared with the Youngstown State University football team, the athletic facilities got their share of use. When someone we knew made a success of themselves, we were never envious, but were proud of their achievements.

For example, Cardinal Mooney High School is less than half a mile from my old high school and being a parochial school lures lots of good athletes from my school to theirs. A few doors up the street from where I lived was one such athlete, John Horney, an All City linebacker from Cardinal Mooney. But once he graduated from Mooney he went on to star in the late 1960s for Ara Parseghian at Notre Dame. He was no longer a neighbor who defected to heated rival Cardinal Mooney; he was John Horney from Cambridge Avenue who played for Notre Dame.

When I first moved to Arizona I was amazed at the facilities available for the youths. Where my house was in Mesa, within a mile there were two junior high schools that had their own football fields complete with grandstands and scoreboards. What was more astounding was that they sat vacant most of the time. In my old high school, the practice field was reduced to dirt and rocks by mid-season. On more than one occasion I recall Tom, myself and other kids from the block getting up a football game in the street on Detroit or Lucius Avenues, which was as we called it "telephone pole to telephone pole," the poles being the goal lines. The outside edges of the sidewalk were the sidelines. Trees, trash cans and parked cars were considered "in play" and would often be used as "picks" are used in basketball. By that I mean that you would run a play or pass pattern in such a manner that the close proximity of the car, trash can or tree would be used as sort of a fixed blocker.

I remember one afternoon we had a game going and I let fly a long pass that would have come down somewhere in the middle of Detroit had it not been for a sudden gust of wind that pushed it slightly from right to left. Given the change in trajectory, the ball and the kid trying to catch it all came to meet right at the left front fender of a 1959 Chevy parked at the curb, where the pass receiver caught it and at the same time made a gut-wrenching "clunk." Surprisingly, neither the ball, the young boy, nor the fender suffered any injury.

Since, this book is about high school football and those who are loyal to it, I do not want to overlook a key individual whom I met in my life who epitomized the devotion to high school football.

I had a neighbor, Bob S. who lived across the street from me on Cambridge. Bob was what we would call in this day and age "mentally challenged," although growing up he was just "Bobby." Well, Bobby's focus in life was the Woodrow Wilson High School football team, especially the junior high football team, and it seemed to be all he lived for. The players on the team could not help but see his love for the athletes and they took the results of the games very seriously. He would come around to practice in all kinds of weather and grill player after player on what they thought would be the outcome of that week's contest.

I remember one week when I was a sophomore, our team suffered a tough loss after a really hard-fought contest and the next day I was out doing some yard work and Bobby came running out of the house and was pleading with me to come up with a reason that we lost such a hard-fought contest, and I didn't even play that night. That did not matter to him; he wanted answers. He had a slight difficulty pronouncing my name and at least ten times he asked, "Warry, what happened last night?"

He was generally admired by the players and I have to admit that there were times that the team would be assembled before a practice and for whatever reason the real coaches would be late in arriving. As players we would kind of elevate Bobby to interim coach status and ask him to give the boys a pep talk.

Whether it was the varsity, JV or junior high, we would all huddle around Bobby and he would muster up as emotional a speech as he could considering his disabilities. We would let Bobby work us up into a frenzy and we would all cheer and break ranks to allow Bobby to pass through as if royalty.

On those occasions, he would be absolutely beaming with pride and enthusiasm that would have made the late Knute Rockne proud.

Evidently, the effort to school Bobby in a traditional fashion had gotten as far as it was going to go and he no longer attended school or the special education classes that were available to him. But, well into his twenties he still continued to come around the high school with the enthusiasm of someone ten years younger.

Then one day, and to this day I can't put my finger on it, I began to notice that Bobby wasn't coming around anymore. I did not see him in the neighborhood either. It was just like he disappeared off the face of the Earth. I would run into one of my pals and say, "Hey, have you seen Bobby S. lately?" and one or more of my buddies would say, "You know now that you mention it, I haven't seen him in the longest time."

As time would go on, I guess even at that young age my peers figured I had an investigative side, so they would come up to me looking for any news on Bobby's absence, but none was forthcoming.

I never had occasion to meet Bobby's parents as they kept to themselves, so there was never explanation as to where he went or when.

I had heard later that Bobby's mental condition worsened and he had to be institutionalized, but that was just a rumor. To this day I never found the reason for Bobby's exit from the neighborhood, but he is one of many individuals who, for whatever reason or another might be gone, but are difficult to forget.

CHAPTER III

GETTING STARTED

Every officiating career has to start somewhere and in my case, officially, it was at Grand Canyon University a long time ago. In those days it was customary for new officials to attend a special rules class separate from the others. Older officials were welcome to attend but the focus of the classes was at the inexperienced newcomers. Most of the older guys just sat off by themselves and heckled the instructors and rookies. For example one of the instructors was trying to explain what one would do when showing up to officiate your first contest. He was saying that you should seek out the crew chief, go up to him and introduce yourself. Explain to him that you are a new official and at that point one of the older wise asses yelled, "And then go home!"

Unofficially, the seeds of the idea were sown back in Ohio in the early '70s. As I've previously mentioned, I'm from Youngstown, Ohio, located in the northeastern part of the state. High school football is hugely popular in that part of the country. I mean not only in the larger metropolitan areas but in the small towns as well. For big schools it would not be unusual to see crowds between 10,000 to 15,000 in attendance. Legendary Massillon Tigers, the home of coaching legend Paul Brown has a high school football stadium that holds over 20,000 and there aren't many empty seats.

One night when I was still a police officer I was assigned patrol the area around South High Stadium on Market Street, one of the two high school football stadiums in town back then. The game that night featured Youngstown Chaney, a regular power in the City Series and Cardinal Mooney, a parochial school that is also a perennial power in the Steel Valley Conference. South High Stadium was in the middle of a business/residential area and did not have a big parking lot and those inside the stadium said it seemed like there were ten thousand people in attendance that night, and although I doubted it there was no way to prove otherwise, but admittedly, there was a huge crowd there that night. Anyways, despite the lack of adequate parking, I envisioned a nightmare as I was the only officer assigned at the time for traffic control. But, in three hours I only had to tow one car that was blocking a garage. Once the game was over the crowd was very orderly and emptied out in less than half an hour.

Anyhow, some schools would utilize newer officials to work the chain crew. It was a good way for the rookies to watch the game up close and watch the experienced officials work. Sometimes they would even pay them five or ten bucks for their trouble. As popular as football is, I would have done it for free (in later years I would), the few bucks being gravy.

After moving here to Arizona and finding myself with evenings and weekends free I thought, *What the hell, why not look into it?* I did and my original intention was to just work the chain crew a few games and maybe see some good football up close. But, for the most part to work the chains you had to do all the requirements of a regular official and it became apparent early on that they expect you to work games as an official, although they initially would be JV or frosh contests. I thought that shouldn't be too bad and for an extra fifteen bucks here and there how bad could it be? Besides, even most of the experienced officials that would talk to me said that the economy was in pretty sorry shape around here and because of that there was no shortage of officials here (this was in the early eighties) and that suited me just fine. I figured with an abundance of experienced officials to work the JV and freshman games and the newer officials very rarely given varsity assignments, how many games could it be?

Well, everyone who thinks that they are a serious football fan is sure that they know the rules of the game. One thing became very clear to me right from the outset. The one thing I found out that I knew about the rules of football is that I didn't know shit about the rules. From what I knew from watching football on Saturdays and Sundays was totally different from what I had to know for Friday nights. For example, I (and probably many others) did not know that the team that is scored upon has the option of kicking or receiving the ensuing kickoff. Do you ever see it? I never did! But just the same that option is available. The rule book is full of lots of strange things that are not commonly known and just because they are not everyday occurrences, in the event they do happen; an official has to know how to apply the rule.

Each night the focus of the class would be on one section of the rule book. One night the entire class will be devoted to "Periods, Time Factors and Substitutions." On another it might be spent entirely on the field dimensions and equipment. So now this is where you start to get the idea that there might be some guys out there that as officials they might take their role a little too seriously. I heard tell of one official who carried around a tire gauge to measure that the game ball had the correct amount of air in it. Another used a less scientific approach. When given the game ball during the pre-game he would just bite on the end and could determine the proper inflation. As the instructor liked to say, "So the ball is a little soft or too hard, what are you gonna do, not play the game?" Along this line, one of my fellow novice officials asked a question that evoked childhood memories.

Allow me to digress a moment. I recall I must have been seven or eight years old, which would have made my older brother Gib fourteen or fifteen, and one Christmas he wanted a football. On that morning he opened one of his presents which was a brand new football. A brand new WHITE football with BLACK stripes. At that point I had never seen such a thing, but this was about 1958 and a lot of high school football stadiums had miserable lighting (you'd be surprised how many still do in 2002) and to aid in visibility a white football was not that uncommon. However, that was the only one I ever saw up close and it didn't prevent me and my brother from having a good old time playing with it.

So now here I am some twenty-three years later and this one guy asks what to do if a team wants to use one of those white footballs. Of course this resulted in rolled eyeballs and hoots from the older officials in attendance, at which point the instructor replied again, "What are you gonna do, not play the game?" which I quickly figured was a nice way of saying, "Just move on!"

As I sat there having rules information being thrown at me in bucketfuls, I figured that the best thing to do was keep my ears open and my mouth shut. I figured that if I had a legitimate question, I could ask after class. Besides, the two instructors had about fifty years' experience between them and covered each chapter in the rule book well enough that it left to me few questions. In the years that followed that also was the case and pretty much whoever the instructor was, he was well-prepared. If the official in attendance would just let the instructors instruct most rules, meetings would flow a lot smoother and we could all get to go home sooner. Now to some people that doesn't sound like a big deal but most rules meetings and clinics are held in August and in this state the daytime temperature hovers well into the triple-digit range, and although an effort is made to cool the rooms, often the heat of the day wins in the long run.

I guess that there are folks who don't mind the heat or maybe they have a grumpy spouse that makes life at home so miserable that they will do anything to drag the time away from them out as long as possible. Maybe there are those who think as football officials they are quite important or just maybe they like the sound of their own voice. Whatever the reason, it seems like there are always one or two individuals who slow the process with ridiculous interruptions.

One of them is the official that has a few years under his belt but feels slighted that he wasn't selected as one of the rules instructors but can't help touting his own knowledge. This usually occurs when the instructor is emphasizing a key point. This is where the teacher wannabe interjects, "Now let that be a lesson to you younger officials." At that point he will have some game experience that he just must describe so the point of emphasis is hammered home indelibly or at least he thinks it is.

Another is the real old timer that can't help but recall how things were done in the "good old days." I have a tremendous amount of respect for my elders and I appreciate the strides and sacrifices made by the older officials who may have made my lot in life as a football official a little easier. But when I am sweating like crazy and my ass is cemented to some seventh grader's desk chair, the fact that penalty flags were preceded by penalty horns and that Monday Night Football is not interrupted by a "horn on the play," just doesn't seem pertinent to me. I am just about not as interested in hearing about how Arizona State University fared in the old Border Conference when they were known as Tempe Normal or whatever name they were back then.

There are some people, no matter how long they are officials, they just don't get it. By that I mean no matter how hard one tries to explain the application of a rule it just doesn't sink in. One night the leader was going over the "false start." Simply stated that means that once the offensive players are set, prior to the snap they cannot make any movements that give the impression that action that one would expect to see at the snap or start of the play has occurred. This particularly applies to offensive lineman who once they are set pretty much cannot move. This seems all pretty much black and white, but as one of my old police instructors said to my class over thirty years ago, when dealing with what seems black and white, there is often a lot of grey. You are dealing with kids when often the range of their skill level varies widely as does their attention span. The younger the player the more that range widens and an official has to recognize that. A ten- or eleven-year-old playing in his first or second youth football game might not have the discipline or grasp of the fundamentals and it is not uncommon for there to be an unintentional flinch as the player is set. The common-sense application is to gauge the situation and as long as neither team is gaining an advantage, keep the flag in your pocket and let the game proceed. The operative phrase there being "common sense." One character that comes to mind didn't see it this way and had a whole laundry list of Pop Warner games that he had officiated where he insisted the infractions had to be penalized. He was not shy about sharing this with the rest of the class, at length, much to the frustration of the instructors and those in attendance. The guy, who bore a striking resemblance to Fred Flintstone, not only didn't get it, he would not shut up. He did however have plenty of opportunities to work Pop Warner games on Saturday mornings since most officials were reluctant to work on Friday nights with such an over-officious bonehead.

As in any walk of life there are the ass-kissers and back-stabbers. I began to think of football officiating as a hobby that you just happened to get paid for. Like any other undertaking one chooses in life, an individual begins as a novice and with time and experience you become more advanced in your skill level. There are those who for whatever reason do not wish to make the necessary effort that one puts into a task to develop into a more progressive individual in that particular endeavor. Instead they choose to curry favor with those who are in a position to aid them in their advancement. In the case of football officiating, that would most likely be those at the local association who assign officials to game and determine which officials will be promoted and which ones will not. It was when I ran across these individuals that I learned early on that there were some colleagues of mine who really took themselves way too seriously in that they had no misgivings about bad mouthing or attacking the reputation of veteran officials to advance their own career. I mean, my God, this is not a Fortune 500 company we are dealing with here; this is high school football. At best it is a fifteen-week season played one game at a time.

Whether I like them or not I always get my game assignments and show up as scheduled and give as good an effort to the two schools as I can. There was a fellow football official who seemed to always be sucking up to the Commissioner or members of his staff and said that he will not work anything but 4-A or 5-A games. These are the two biggest divisions in the state and sure as shit when the schedule came out he was working all the big games. I seldom griped about it for two reasons. The first one was that my fellow officials have eyes and TV sets as well as I do and every week when the local cable company played the tape-delayed broadcasts of the week's big games there was this big oaf on the tube. It doesn't take long for the word to get around that this guy was hand-picking his own games or so it seemed. The second reason was that the game fee for a big game and a little school is the same, so all his ass-kissing did was increase his exposure but not his pocketbook.

There were not many who shared the same thoughts as I and some expressed their frustration by refusing to sign up the following season and some good officials were lost as a result. It seemed that the powers that be did not see this as a serious problem because the supply of new officials seemed endless so nothing was done to rectify the situation. Of course no one would admit that there was any favoritism although the rank and file thought otherwise.

The absolute last straw for some came from of all places baseball. Supposedly this official was also a baseball umpire and in the spring when discussing the next fall this guy said in the presence of a few other football officials that he was guaranteed a State Championship the following year. Word of that spread like wildfire and the following season when that same official and his crew ended up working a State Final, a lot of my fellow officials were fit to be tied. I must admit I was beginning to share in some of that frustration until our back judge Mark Ostreicher said as he had many times, "You know they may be getting bigger games than us but I doubt if they are having as much fun."

Another example came when the working officials were at odds with the head of the Observer program, a group that evaluates each crew. One official would come to meetings and bad mouth the head of that program and would sit in a bar with us and say how he thought the guy was a big blowhard and disparage the whole program, calling it a mockery and a waste of time.

That year our crew was doing a game at a Scottsdale High School and one of our guys goes up to the press box to talk to the clock operator before the game only to return and inform us that the head of the Observers is up there with his binoculars, and who is sitting right by his side all nice and sociable but none other than our fellow official who was scoffing at him a few nights ago.

When you become a football official, you learn to look at football differently and you learn a few things you didn't before, and you will experience a few changes.

A football-officiating career is not going to make you rich, with game fees ranging between twenty-five to fifty dollars a game. As a football official you are going to have to give up a great deal of your free time between travel to and from games, kickoff and rules clinics, mechanics clinics, scrimmages and seminars. As a matter of fact, one time about four or five years ago I worked a game and our crew had the occasion to have an Observer present. An Observer is usually a retired official that volunteers to go out to games and watch crews work and then submit an evaluation form on the crew's performance. At the time an adverse Observer's evaluation could cost a crew a playoff game; although the powers that be denied it, experience taught me otherwise. I will expand on the Observer program later on. In any event, the Observer on this night was a man who many years ago taught me how to be a football umpire, a position (right behind the defense) that if you don't know what you are doing can at the least seriously disrupt the flow of the game and more seriously can get you hurt. This guy is also one of the toughest sons of bitches I ever met, and I've met a few. After having part of one leg amputated after suffering a blood clot, he continues to golf in handicap Olympics and probably can still get out there on Friday nights but by his own admission has nothing to prove. Anyway, after the game we invited him to join us for a bite to eat. He told us that when he was an active official, at the end of each football season, he had his own method of evaluating just how successful the previous season actually was. His theory was that if you spent more money on post game pizzas and beer than you took in as game fees then the season was a success.

You learn that as an official you sort of acquire a different alphabet. The ABC's you learned as a youngster becomes *A's, B's, K's and R's*. To converse among experienced officials and more importantly to understand high school football publications such as rule books, case books, official's manuals and tests, you must develop a new lingo so to speak. The team on offense is referred to as team A and the defense is team B. The team that is kicking the football is K and obviously the receiving team is R. Thus, when a team punts the ball downfield and one of the opposition's players signals for and makes a fair catch, it will now be described as, "K's scrimmage kick is in flight when player R1 who is on R's side of the line signals for and makes a fair catch." Simple eh?

Part of the start-up process involves purchasing the equipment you need to go out and do a game. There are several outfits that specialize in offering official's gear for sale and you can get it through mail order and more recently make your purchases online with your home computer. There are sporting goods stores that also offer some of the equipment and that works well if you need a last-minute item, but the stores that specialize exclusively seem to me to have a bigger selection. Now there are obvious things you are going to need such as striped shirts, knickers, shorts, etc. but there are little things you need to help you to do your job properly. For instance, you need a game card to keep track of penalties, time-outs, captain's numbers, who won the coin toss and the ball position at the end of the first and third quarters when you switch ends of the field. They sell special belts that keep your referee's shirt from becoming untucked during a game. As an umpire you usually spot the ball after each play and all that bending over will cause your shirt to come out in no time.

In purchasing official's equipment you can really knock yourself out with gadgets. There are some items you will need that you should spend some time and money on your purchase and others you don't. Most important is a good pair of shoes. If you are going to be on your feet for two and a half hours you are going to have a miserable time if your feet hurt or you get a blister. As the season drags on some fields get as hard as the track that surrounds them, so get shoes that have some padding. And if you are an umpire, make sure the shoes have strong upper construction because sooner or later some kid is going to step on you and in my case it was seldom the lightest player on the field. It usually was some big defensive lineman and in each case they were immediately sorry, but that didn't stop my foot from hurting like hell.

The least investment you should make is in the penalty flag. For years I carried a yellow cloth napkin with a small rock wrapped in the middle for weight. Now here is where you might find some folks that take this stuff too seriously. I was always leery about an official if when I worked with him for the first time and he shows up with a penalty flag hanging out of his right back pocket, another hanging out of the left and two more tucked into his belt. Does he intend to throw all four on one play?

One of the veteran officials who got my early respect once told me, "Bury that damn flag as deep in your pocket as you can so that it is not easy for you to get to and just throw it whenever you feel like it!" His approach was that you are not just tossing yellow hankies around, but rather you are part of the teaching process; it is "high school" sports after all. You should talk with the players on the little stuff to avoid penalties because after all it does slow down the game. Rather than ding a kid for lining up a little offside, just warn them on the next play to watch where they're lining up. Don't let them know they got away with one, but plant the seed in their mind that you are watching them. The same goes for holding. Most good coaches will tell their player that if someone is doing something illegal to tell an official. If a player came up to me and complained of holding or any other infraction I would usually try to get a number. If I could, then on the ensuing down I would stand over the line where he would line up before the play would start. I would then address that whole side of the formation that they were getting sloppy, to clean it up and that I would be watching and it would work the majority of the time.

One official I met who I didn't hold in too high regard used to boast that he just kept the tip of his flag in his back pocket and leave most of it dangling out because, as he puts it, "I want them to really see it so it can be a constant reminder of what could happen if they screw up, and I'll toss it in a heartbeat." If this guy was around then I'll bet he was really demoralized when they changed the flag color from red to yellow.

The rules meetings that first season were nearing completion and we were preparing to take our rules test. Besides the meetings, we were required to attend mechanics clinics. What those are, are when careful attention is given to where each position should be prior to the ball being snapped and then where to position yourself during a play or game situation. This is done with videos and then on-the-field simulations. They take you from the pre-game conference, the coin toss, game situations, duties at the end of a quarter and the end of a half or game. Even though I figured I would only get a few actual games to officiate, I paid particular attention to the instructors. One reason was that although I might not officiate too many games, as a fair-skinned Slovak I turn red easily and am not in the habit of making too much of a fool of myself. Another reason was that the officials conducting the mechanics clinic looked to have put forth considerable time and effort into the class and that it would be terribly disrespectful to act like a jackass as few of the classmates were doing. Years later I would serve on the board of the local association and prove my theory correct when I would get a chance to see just how tirelessly these officials would work to put on these clinics and the whole behind-the-scenes lengths they go to in trying to get all the officials to work as a unit and look professional in the process.

It was about this time I began to feel that no amount of classroom time or clinics would prepare me for what takes place on a football field during a game. I seemed to recall during my high school days that we would have scrimmages between other schools and there were officials in attendance, so I was sure that was the case in Arizona and it turned out that I figured correctly. I spoke with one of the instructors and he said that there would be opportunities to work pre-season scrimmages and that they would rotate the new officials in with the experienced ones. He even told me that there were several scrimmages in which the experienced officials were the instructors and mechanics clinic committee so as not to feel intimidated by some of the older, more aloof officials. In fact, there was one coming up in a few days and was told I could attend if I wanted to.

My first scrimmage was at Alhambra High School and the temperature was around 109 degrees. So I put on my brand-spanking-new official's outfit complete with white shorts (we're allowed to wear shorts for most games with the exception of varsity night games) and set out for Alhambra. I figured this would give me a good opportunity to get some work in since I had the initiative to ask and maybe not too many other officials there did.

I seriously underestimated the initiative of my fellow rookies because when I pulled into the parking lot and looked out onto the football field I saw what looked like about thirty officials out there. Well so much for getting any serious field time, but I went on in anyway.

This was just a scrimmage between Alhambra players only and it would be run in series of ten plays for each side. We were told that the experienced officials were taking the first series and after a short break the rookies could rotate in their place for a few plays and take turns until all got a chance to participate. We were urged to try a few plays at each position: linesman, line judge, referee and umpire (we didn't start using back judges until years later).

So, things got going and I watched the older officials out there. For the two sideline officials, the linesman and line judge, there were eight to ten guys lined up waiting to get in, and the same for the "White Hat," the referee. As I surveyed the field I saw there was nobody waiting to rotate in at the umpire's position. I figured at least I could get some work in there so I wandered out to the middle of the field after the first ten play series. The guy that was the umpire came up to me and I told him I was new and he gave a brief orientation. He told me to stay between the hash marks and to line up three to seven yards behind the ball. It was my responsibility to spot the ball and mark off penalties (maybe I should have studied the penalty part of the rule book a little better) and count the defense. I'm sure he told me much more but my brain was racing and that's all that sank in at the time.

So the plays start and there are players flying all over the place. They are running by me, at me, into me and around me. If there were any fouls I didn't see them because I was trying not to get killed. No wonder there was no one else anxious to get at the umpire position; you would have to be crazy to insert yourself in the middle of all this chaos. Remember, the kids have pads and helmets; I don't. I wanted to get the hell out of there, and go stand in the line with all the others to work as a linesman or line judge, way out there by the SIDELINE! So as soon as the real umpire returned I was going to thank him for the opportunity and get out of Dodge. After the ten play series, he told me what I did wrong, but I don't remember what it was. But he did a real mean thing to me; he left me in there for more opportunities to get killed.

So I had no choice but to get back in there; I couldn't just walk off the job and look like a coward. After a couple more plays something happened and somewhere way back in the rubbish heap I call my brain I recalled that I did play some football or at least I went to practice. Anyhow, I started remembering some of the basic football fundamentals. Simple stuff like, if at the snap the offensive linemen step back into a pass blocking stance, it's probably going to be a pass. In the confused mass of information that had been thrown at me during the hours of rules meetings and mechanics clinics, a single bit of information came to the surface. If it's a pass play, the umpire must step forward to the line of scrimmage to make sure no linemen go downfield illegally and that a forward pass crosses the line of scrimmage. The next time they dropped back into the pass blocking stance I worked my way forward to the line of scrimmage. Nothing went wrong, but I thought at least if it did I was where I was supposed to be, a fact that did not go unnoticed by the veteran official I was standing in for. Again, the guard pulls it most likely is a sweep. Whichever direction the guard goes it's pretty likely that is where the sweep is headed and it is probably a good idea to rotate away from it unless you want to get trampled. I learned in later years that that is not usually a failsafe routine and not to relax because just about that time they will run a trap play or reverse and you're face-to-face with a ball carrier looming down on you like a locomotive. I later learned that if you are an umpire you are going to get knocked on your ass from time to time.

The truth be known now, for years I had a boss at my regular job who was a real horse's ass and was on my ass constantly for the most picayune of reasons. An example was that we operated a small fleet of vehicles of the hospital security force I was a supervisor at. One day the ignition switch crapped out on one of the Toyota vehicles we used to patrol the property. (Up until the time he took over we mostly drove American-made vehicles.) The car was taken to a local dealership for the repairs and we were told that it would be several days before the car could be repaired because there was not a single ignition switch for that model of auto in the entire Phoenix area and one would have to be special ordered from out of state. The next morning when he saw that this particular vehicle was not in service, he proceeded to launch into a tirade in front of at least one other co-worker which infuriated the hell out of me. What was I supposed to do, wave a magic wand and make an ignition switch appear out of nowhere? Anyways, it was after exchanges such as these I would be working a game and purposely put myself in harm's way and have a lineman or linebacker barreling down on me and rather than get out of the way I would plant my feet and throw a shoulder into him. Obviously, he is wearing all kinds of padding and no way I was going to hurt him, but boy oh boy, would that help relieve the stress. Usually the player would check afterwards to make sure he knew where I was.

I actually found myself staying out of harm's way and didn't feel as terrified and started to get a handle on what was happening around me, albeit a small handle. One the last play of that ten play series I think it was a sweep to the left and off to the right I saw it. An offensive lineman had his arm wrapped around a defender and a handful of jersey. I reached into my pocket and pulled out my new flag and let it rip. I told the ref what I had, marched off the yards and ran one more play. During the break the real umpire called me aside to critique my performance. He didn't so much say my penalty call was bad but he emphasized that the foul was away from the play and had no effect on the outcome. If this had been a game situation it might have been better to leave the flag in my pocket and between plays say to the offender that I'd be watching him or "keep it clean." Then if he continued to do it then flag him. Don't tell him what he did or he'd feel he got away with one. We are there to help teach, not to take officiating too seriously and to over-officiate. He also told me the best compliment an official can receive is when you walk off the field after a game and to have someone say to you, "We didn't even know you guys were out there." I took that advice with me my entire career.

Well, I settled in and he let me umpire the rest of the scrimmage, sometimes with him standing right behind me so he was seeing what I was seeing and offering me periodic advice. I must have settled in pretty well because I remained as an umpire for most of the next twenty-two years, but the experience of that first scrimmage and the advice stuck with me the rest of my career.

A while later I get a letter in my mailbox with my game assignments in it. The three or four games I thought I would get turned out to be eleven JV and frosh games, two of which were on the same night at 4:00 and 6:00. This happened to be on my wedding anniversary, a fact that did not sit well with my first wife. I actually only got to work three or four chain crews. When the association sends your game assignments, copies are sent to the schools so they can pay you. The level an official is ranked determines how much you get paid. A newer official, a level four, might get $12.00 a game where a veteran, a level one, might get $15.00 for a JV/frosh game. The coaches also see the assignment sheet and if they see a level four newer official working their game, there are a few who see that as an opportunity to ride the hell out of you or try to influence your calls. You learn real quickly to tune out this sort of behavior; those that can't are called "rabbit ears."

When I first started we didn't use crews so I found myself working with different officials just about every contest. That taught me a lot about being the new kid on the block and how to treat other new kids once I became experienced. It is best to just tell who you are working with that you're new. They had to have been new once and most of them will understand and try to help you out. If they ask, tell them a little about yourself. Be brief, even after you've been around awhile. Remember, a little humility goes a long way. Every official makes a mistake, but the last thing you need is to show up with some crew you've never worked with before and shoot your mouth off about what a great official you are and then go make a jackass call or two.

Once the game is over, listen to the critique of your performance and don't take it personally. If you are the one doing the critique, be honest but do it tactfully. Don't tell an official he did a good job and then fill out the evaluation form (if there is one) and tear him apart. Our state used to have an evaluation form that the experienced official would have to fill out and mail in. I used to go as far as giving them a stamped envelope so there was no excuse for them not to mail it in. In order to move up a level we used to have to have a minimum number of evaluations, so the more that were sent in the better chances of moving up. I figured any evaluation, even a bad one was better than not having any at all.

On one such occasion I did a game and it was one of the rare games where I was the line judge. I gave the referee my form and envelope with hopes he would send it in. He did and in fact he ripped me apart. The Commissioner went as far as to send me a copy of it along with a note that I would have to do better. Not the sort of thing you want in your file if you want to get moved up. But, once I read the evaluation's comments, it was clear he had me mistaken for my counterpart across the field, the line judge because the comments had to do with miscommunications with the chain crew and messing up the down box numerous times which was his responsibility. He, too, was a newer official and must have had him fill one out and he got us confused.

In later years, I found myself in the position of being the veteran official and being asked to evaluate an official's performance and for that reason I would take the time to recognize the guy or gal's job and do it accurately.

CHAPTER IV

GETTING THERE

Before you can officiate a contest you have to get there in one piece. Sometimes that can present challenges from time to time. For varsity contests usually the travel arrangements are made by the crew chief unless they can't handle the task and then it is delegated to one of the other team members.

Since most games are on Friday nights, to get to your assigned contest requires trying to negotiate through rush hour traffic. No easy task in the metro Phoenix area where there isn't an abundance of freeways and early evening accidents clogging them are common place.

Early on I mentioned Elmer and initially he wanted to do the driving. He drove a circa 1977 Gremlin station wagon with a plastic drop cloth draped between the back seat and the rear portion of the wagon. I think this was an attempt to cut down on cooling costs by not allowing the cool air to circulate into the rear part of the car. Elmer and Harry used to ride in the front and Roger and I would ride in the back seat. Comfort-wise this did not sit too well with me because there are few passenger cars that have back seats that can accommodate a person over six feet tall, let alone a seventies version

Gremlin wagon. But in those days Roger and I used to smoke so Roger and I would sit in the back seat and smoke our brains out while Harry would have to sit up front and listen to Elmer gripe about his lack of big game assignments or the miserable treatment he was getting from the official's association.

On one memorable trip to Buckeye, a town about sixty miles west of town, we were zipping down I-10 doing about seventy and Roger and I were sitting in the back smoking like chimneys, and Elmer was in one of his tirades. Did I mention that when he would launch into one of these tirades that his attention was severely diminished? So we were approaching a point where I-10 narrowed from three lanes to two. The state placed "rumble strips" in the right hand lane of the highway to warn motorists in the lane that was soon to vanish. Elmer actually turned to face us in the back seat to drive home a point as we approached the warning bumps and it sounded something like this: "Ya know when Sid Grandy was Commissioner," KA-THUMP-THUMP-THUMP, "I used to get all the big games," KA-THUMP-THUMP-THUMP. We were screaming because the lane we were traveling in was about to be replaced by a bridge abutment which was dead in our path at seventy miles an hour. Finally at the last moment we got him to focus his attention on the road ahead and at the last second he veered into the appropriate lane, narrowly averting a crash.

The adventure did not end there. To get to the town of Buckeye from I-10 you have to travel down a two lane highway for five or ten miles. Every so often you see white crosses by the roadside indicating that some motorist(s) have had an accident with fatal results. Clearly, vigilance is a good thing to have on this stretch of road. So we were zipping down the highway doing about sixty now. From the back seat we could see that there was a four-way stop sign up ahead; unfortunately, our driver who was yet in another harangue about the shoddy treatment he was getting, did not see it and he flew right through it. Luckily, there was no traffic coming. By this time we had implored him to pay more attention so we wouldn't get killed. So a little further down the road we felt the car easing to a stop, so I figured another four-way stop. We looked up but there was no stop sign and no crossing traffic either. He just for no reason stopped in the middle of the intersection. Through the plastic drop cloth we could see a tractor-trailer pulling a cotton module approaching rapidly from behind doing about sixty. Now we were trying to get him to get moving because those tractor-trailers can't stop on a dime.

When the game was over, which was about 11:00 p.m. on the drive back Elmer broke out his sunglasses for the return trip back to town because the glare of oncoming headlamps annoyed him.

It was after that trip that we decided that anyone other than Elmer would do the driving. Since it was apparent at the time that we would be doing a lot of out of town travel, we had to make plans each week to meet at a location that would at least put us on a side of town that was in the direction we were headed and each of us lived on a different side of town. Obviously out of town games require more travel time and adjustments have to be made, including dietary ones. Now I prefer not to eat within four hours before a game, but I am more the exception than the rule. For a few years we had a guy who worked with us that was into health foods. We had a game in Kearny, a little mining town nestled in the mountains about seventy-five miles southeast of town. We met at a mutually convenient location and this guy said he would provide the pre-game meals. As usual I declined the offer but Roger had this hamburger concoction made out of soybeans, some kind of "soy-burger." Whatever was in it did not sit well with him because he got a case of diarrhea like you wouldn't believe. It was a good thing we were traveling in a motor home with a bathroom in it because two-thirds of the way there he went inside and didn't come out until we got to Kearny.

When we got to the school, the game administration escorted us to the dressing area and he went in the men's room and was in and out right up until game time. We thought we might have to do the game with three officials. It's hard enough to do a game with four officials let alone three. But somehow he was able to tough it out and got through it okay. After that, no more health food or soy-burgers. I continued my pre-game fasting ritual. More recently, my idea of a pre-game meal consists of an energy bar and a jug of Gatorade.

When you're dealing with motor vehicles I guess sooner or later you're going to endure mechanical difficulties. On a trip to one game we gassed up Harry's mobile home for a trip of about twenty-five miles. We smelled gasoline right off the bat but attributed that to the recent fueling. But as we proceeded the smell lingered and got stronger as we went on. We all figured a gas tank leak (none of us are mechanics) but once we got to Cave Creek could not find any gas puddles. We did the game and when it was over checked again but found nothing. When we drove back there was the smell again. We later learned that it was a problem with the fuel pump. It was pumping gas to the engine but also pumping an equal amount under the passenger compartment and on the road. By that time we had quit smoking.

Before you get to the game you have to pack your equipment. In the early years I used to be fanatical about packing my bag to the point that I would put the bag in the trunk of my car and then go down and check it four or five times before I had to leave to make sure I had everything. In later years I became a little complacent but for the most part never forgot anything major. As a crew we wholeheartedly agreed that the one thing we should never leave home was Hank Morris. Hank is a nurse at J.C. Lincoln hospital and for the last ten years or so has been the linesman. Hank brings two of everything. Yes, including jock straps. Not everyone on our crew is the same size as Hank, but if something doesn't fit you just have to make do.

Last year we were in Cave Creek again. I still packed my own bag and at that time we just started using the placards. Those are the big letters you see on the back of official's shirts on college games (R for referee, B for back judge, etc.). My fiancé used to wash my shirt by hand and let it hang dry so the placard won't get wrinkled or damaged. Somehow, I forgot that the shirt was hanging in the closet while the rest of my stuff was folded in the laundry basket. Anyway, I got all the way to the school and no striped shirt. Our Commissioner at the time lived not too far from Cave Creek and had a habit of dropping in unannounced at their home games to watch the crews work their games. So I couldn't just walk out there with no shirt although it was early in the year and hotter than hell. Hank to the rescue; he had an extra shirt and an extra set of placards, but it was a large and I wear an extra-large. I had been bragging before the season that I had lost weight as I do every year, but this year I really felt like I had. I went to put on Hank's shirt and much to everyone's surprise it fit. So, for a moment I was panicked that the Commissioner might show up, then I felt good because I can't recall the last time I fit into a size large. My best estimate was that that occurred sometime during a year that began with a 197.

As bad as forgetting my shirt is, it does not compare to what happened to Roger one night. At the time he had a condo in central Phoenix not far from the Biltmore, and we were scheduled to do a game at Thunderbird High. It was a distance of about ten miles. Not a great distance, but it required driving right through the city's central corridor during rush hour when traffic moves sometimes at a snail's pace. I met him at his condo and parked my truck in his carport and we start making our way to the game. Thunderbird had at the time a new coach and there were some reports that he and his staff had been pretty tough on a few crews in previous contests. It's not as if we haven't had to deal with difficult coaches in the past, but Roger had a friend at Thunderbird and during the week got the lowdown. He was told that the coach was a young guy who was a little intense but in no way a poor sport or one to berate officials. It may have been just that maybe one of the crews overreacted, which could be the case. We had done a lot of games at Thunderbird and not had any problems before.

About a half mile from the school we were just moving right along and could see the football field lights up ahead when he hollered "Oh shit!" and pulled into a parking lot. He grabbed his keys, ran to the back of the car and opened the trunk. It looked kind of empty with only my equipment bag back there. He had left his bag at the house. In those days we did not have Hank on our crew with two of everything. So he dropped me off at the school and began to head back. It was about six and we left at five o'clock or just about a little less than an hour to cover ten miles. I went in the dressing room and there were the other two guys because something else we did not have at the time was a back judge or a fifth man. I told Harry he might want to dig out his white hat since he was Roger's replacement if he missed a game or went down with an injury. We were preparing to do the game with three officials when in strutted three more guys in official's gear. They were our chain crew, all rookie officials.

It was early in the season so we asked if they had done any games at all. I think the most experienced of the bunch had done something like two JV or freshman games and a couple of Pop Warner contests. It is tough enough to do a high school game with four officials, let alone three, especially when it's 100-plus degrees outside. "So this must be your lucky day," we tell the rookie, "you get to be a varsity official and you didn't have to wait four years to do it." All the color kind of ran out of his face and he asked if we were serious. We told him we were indeed serious and as soon as we got dressed there was going to be a pre-game so he better listen up. Really, had we had to press him into service we would have put him on the side with the chains and that alone would have kept him busy all night. Luckily, Roger made it home and back in time for opening kickoff. The rush hour gods must like football officials.

To get to where you're going you should know where it is you're supposed to be. My first year in Arizona the Association tried to round up as many of the first- and second-year officials to work the chain crews for the playoff games as often as possible. Chain crew members were paid fifteen to twenty bucks a game and the thinking behind was that first year officials have the initial expense of purchasing all new uniforms and equipment and this was a nice way of getting them a few extra bucks to help offset that expense.

There are a few high schools that have similar sounding names. Such examples are Desert Ridge, Desert Mountain, Sunrise Mountain, Mountain Ridge, two Mountain Views, Shadow Mountain, and Mountain Point just to name a few. A lot of playoffs are played at neutral sites. So I got a call from the AIA on a Thursday asking if I could work a playoff game the next night. I didn't have much going on and I said I would. I didn't get the name of the schools as much as I did the site, which I was sure they said was off 51st Avenue in the then small city of Glendale. One of the schools was a "Mountain" something. But in those days the City of Glendale had not yet experienced the massive growth explosion that has taken over the whole metro area now. One other piece of information I do recall is that I was told the neutral site was not at Glendale High School.

The next day I was talking to a guy I worked with Jim Hamilton who followed sports pretty well, especially high school. Jim's wife worked in the athletic department at Phoenix College where a lot of local scholastic athletes ended up sooner or later. He asked me if I was working any of the games that night and I told him what I knew. He said that that was probably something like South Mountain and Gilbert being played at Glendale Community College. I asked him where that was located. He told me that GCC was on Dunlap and either 51st or 59th Avenue in Glendale. So, I figured that was it.

During that day there was an unbelievable amount of rain in the span of a few hours, which flooded intersections and washed out freeway underpasses. There was talk of canceling a few of the high school playoff games because fields were underwater or some of the schools may not be able to get their buses to the sites. At about three o'clock that afternoon I called GCC and they said they were in fact hosting a playoff game and as far as the gal I spoke with knew, the game would be played. At the time I felt pretty confident that I was headed in the right direction.

After work I followed Jim's directions to GCC since I hadn't been there before. I was one of the first to arrive and since they just called me about the game I had no assignment sheet with the names of whom I was working with. One by one officials began to arrive, both the game officials and the chain crew. I was about half dressed and some more officials kept arriving so I started to do the math. I counted nine officials in all. So let's see there are the four actually working the game and four more for the chain crew which obviously, added up to eight. I was discussing this fact with one of the other guys assigned to the chain crew. We figured they ought to be in soon with the checks and whoever didn't get a check was the odd man out. One of the guys assigned to work the game was a veteran and said that that was not the case since playoff game checks come in the mail a few weeks after.

All of a sudden I wasn't feeling so confident that I was in the right place. While attending classes for rookie officials, one thing they hammered home was that to not honor an assignment for a game was a cardinal sin. No matter what the excuse, to just not show up for a game would not be tolerated unless, as one instructor liked to say, "You're in a box carried by six of your friends!"

It became clear to me that the nine of us there at GCC were more than enough bodies to work the contest and that somewhere else they were a body short, that body most likely being mine. All I could envision was that on Monday morning some crew chief would be calling the Commissioner's office, telling him, "Whoever this Larry Kovac guy is, never assign him to one of my contests again since he failed to show up for Friday night's game at (insert name of high school here)."

I began to poll the crew members to see if they had any idea where I was supposed to be at. Several of them figured that the closest game in the area was St. Mary's vs. Shadow Mountain at Deer Valley High School. Great, another school I had never heard of, now where the hell is that? I learned that it was a brand new school on 53rd Avenue and Union Hills Road, a location about ten miles north of where I was at. I was already dressed to take the field so I grabbed my street clothes, stuffed them into my equipment bag and hustled back to my car. I began driving north on 59th Avenue, although at the time I lost my bearings and thought I was back down on 51st Avenue. In the area, 51st and 59th Avenues are main streets and cross most of the city uninterrupted and for the most part any major street that crossed 51st crossed 59th as well.

I had been driving for a while and figured I ought to be getting close. I don't recall where I was exactly but the intersection was blocked by the police because it was flooded. They directed me to the west and, thinking I was on 51st, then I shouldn't have been too far off. It was fast approaching seven o'clock and the game, if there was one would be starting in a little more than a half hour. Up ahead I could make out the outline of a big school. There was a football field but it was dark and deserted. I stopped at a convenience store. I was at 67th Avenue and Greenway, not far from Cactus High School and all I had to do was go north on 67th Avenue about two miles to Union Hills, go right about ten blocks and there I would be.

I got there a few minutes after seven o'clock just as they were taking the field. To this day I don't recall the crew chief but he was under the impression that one of the chain crew members was a last minute no show and that they would just have to get by, but now he was glad I was there. I was sweating it for nothing because they had no idea I was even supposed to be there. But I knew I almost messed up and in later years learned that a few minutes to call a school and verify assignment info (most of them call you now) can save you a lot of grief down the road.

Having worked with the same guys for years, when we travel there are not a lot of secrets unless there is some good gossip. But, when we go on the road, it is good natured needling and guy talk among friends. Every once in a while you find yourself subbing for another crew or having someone sub on ours. Now I try to make a point of not tooting my own horn and as I said earlier humility is a good thing. A bunch of total strangers probably don't give a rat's ass that it is November and I just broke up with my girlfriend. The guys I that have known me for many years do, however. They steadfastly maintain that I do it on purpose because they think I'm cheap, not wanting to buy a Christmas present and will get back together after the holidays. They usually have a good time doing so. In any event I try to just listen and if they ask me something or try to make small talk, to be brief unless they ask me to elaborate. Some crew chiefs try to have a pre-game briefing and although we seldom don't while on the road I still listen attentively. This is another instance when they put considerable effort into it and they deserve that degree of respect.

Now one of the things about getting there is what you do before you get to your contest. As a sports official one has to be careful that you don't give your detractors any further ammunition to tear at you, especially if they blame you for their loss. Now I like my cold beer as much as any guy but on game days it is no way, no how, not even a drop. We have worked together for so long we know that each of us adheres to that rule without exception. Many years ago we had a guy who worked with us briefly as a substitute and we all thought he was a capable official. After Elmer's retirement he joined us as a regular. One night I was giving him a ride to a game and it was one of those rare evenings in the Phoenix area where we made exceptional time in getting to our contest. The game was between two very small schools, but even though they were small schools, the rivalry is friendly and intense. We arrived before even the game administration and while we were waiting he suggested we go for a few drinks to kill the time... I thought this was absolutely out of the question and asked if he was out of his mind. His suggestion was if we had a few drinks with vodka in it nobody would know since he bought into the myth that vodka didn't have a distinctive odor. I thought to myself that a few traffic cops and emergency room nurses would tend to disagree.

I didn't say a word but he must have seen the look of utter shock on my face because he then asked if he could go for a drink while I sit there and drink soda. I don't know if it dawned on him, I told him, but possible spectators might be in that bar before the game and it might not look like soda to them and I didn't need the grief. He then tried to blow it off and said he was just kidding, sort of just testing me, but I think I knew better. We started noticing other little chinks in his armor as the season went forward, like arriving the last minute for contests or spans of inattention. During one contest on a particularly hot Saturday afternoon, a close contest at that, he kept imploring Roger to speed up the game since he had other things to do. Of course he accommodated him by being very calm and deliberate, thus adding about another thirty minutes to the contest. He even called for a measurement when it was clear the line to gain was short just to make him drag the chain crew all the way across the field if for no other reason than to piss him off. Once the season was over it was suggested to him he might be better off with another crew.

CHAPTER V

WE'RE HERE!

The officials arrive at their destination and upon their arrival have to find the dressing area. Mostly that means finding the guy with the key. This is someone from the school designated to escort you to the dressing area and then let you in there. The guys with the key can be just about anybody. It can be an athletic director, custodian, security officer, groundskeeper and everyone in between. There was an unconfirmed report that in Florence, the home to Arizona's largest prison, the groundskeeper/guy with the key is a prison trustee. The guy with the key usually has a bunch of other duties given the state of public schools staffing these days. That means that more than likely he'll be doing that when you arrive so you have to wait until they locate him. How long you have to wait seems to get greater the more behind schedule you are.

Most schools do a good job of providing escorts and protection for the officials, but there are those that do the minimum. One school had the guy with the key escort us to a room buried in the bowels of the campus. He unlocked the door and turned on the light. He then told us that when we took the field to pull the door shut when we leave since the door will lock behind us. After that we were pretty much on our own.

School campuses keep getting larger these days and in some cases the official's dressing room keeps getting further away. In some cases they need a golf cart or van to shuttle them back and forth because it is so far away.

One inner city school that has its share of gang problems has the guy with the key meet you at the driveway! From there they take you to a fenced enclosure where they lock your car inside. Nearby is a van that goes to the locker room and stays there until you are ready to take the field, and they drive you there. The van stays at the field and at halftime they give the option of going back to the locker room or sitting in the air conditioned van the entire half. They take you back to the locker room once the game is over and then back to your car. They then follow you off campus and then lock a gate behind you.

Some schools make a tradition of opening their campus to visitors and pride themselves on making the experience for players, fans and referee a pleasant one.

One such school that comes to mind is Paradise Valley High School in northeast Phoenix. When the officials arrive someone from the school is in the parking lot awaiting the arrival. They greet you and hand you a Styrofoam container with your name on it. They escort the official to the dressing room and once you get settled the AD comes in with fresh, clean towels and the game checks. He usually will tell you if they have a chain crew and that the clock operator is experienced and if you need anything ask for him directly. Inside the Styrofoam container you can expect to find sodas, sports drinks and assorted snacks. For a time I used to do Pop Warner games at that school on Saturday mornings and someone there explained it to me why they did that. Someone mentioned that the officials have usually just come straight from work, are tired and haven't eaten since lunch. They thought it would be a nice touch to give them some snacks and beverages to hold them over. They do not expect any preferential treatment and I believe they are sincere in that regard because over the years the staff has changed but the treatment has not. I must say that many schools have adopted various versions of this tradition and maybe officials may not say so often enough but we sure appreciate the gesture.

I remember someone saying something to the effect of, "The only thing people remember more than good service is bad service." The same goes for the officials. Most schools do a good job considering the resources they have to work with these days. But, just as the inside of a home reflects on the occupants, the same can be said for the condition they leave some of their coaches' offices and dressing rooms.

One school let us into their coaches' office to change and on the floor was a dead cricket the size of a silver dollar, which in itself is not too bad, but the cricket was being dragged off by a sewer cockroach about three inches long. Other schools have housed us in quarters so cramped you can barely turn around let alone change, or in a room with one shower for five officials.

I understand with education being what it is that facilities are old and funds are few to make changes. But one suburban school which is neither put us in a locker room that was still under construction and had no running water or toilets. The next year they put us in what amounted to a glorified closet where the hot water heater was located.

Some schools drop the ball right from the start. One year Roger and I were scheduled to do a JV game at high school in Mesa. For the most part we arrived for those games already dressed. We parked our car in the lot south of the field and were walking to the field. As we did I noticed about a half dozen varsity football players walk past us headed in the direction of the car. I realized I had left my whistle in the car and asked Roger for his keys. I turned to walk back to the car and was face-to-face with one of the varsity players who half looked at me and in the direction of our car. He stammered for a moment and then asked me for the time. I continued to walk back to the car and four or five more of the players were walking back to the field. When I got there the passenger side of the car had been keyed and a swastika carved into the trunk lid. Although I had a pretty good idea who was responsible for the damage, I've been around the criminal justice system enough to know that if I didn't see who did it, that was that. I didn't let that stop me from calling the school administration the next day and telling them that I would never do a game at that school again, and I haven't.

I know that the schools are supposed to supply towels for the officials to shower with. I personally bring my own. If a school cares so little about its image that they allow visitors, i.e. officials, to stay in a room that looks awful, how clean can the towels be? Also, every so often the school administration is so busy after a game they just flat out forget to bring towels, so just to be on the safe side I bring mine.

So we were there and found the guy with the key and our dressing room. Usually Roger and I went to meet the coaches before we got dressed. A few years ago Roger attended a referees' seminar and one of the things they covered was going to meet the coach in your street clothes if at all possible. The thinking behind that was that it gave them the opportunity to see the officials as normal guys and not authority figures that can't wait to toss yellow hankies all over the place.

It is necessary for the coach to verify that his players are properly equipped to the referee and me, as they recommend there be a second official there as a witness. As an umpire it is your responsibility to rule on any equipment questions so it just makes good sense that I go along anyway. Most equipment rulings are pretty routine. Usually some player has a cast that needs to be covered, something like that. The last few years there has been an emphasis on knee braces. Now I can say from personal experience that some of these newer knee braces are really remarkable devices. My own knees are pretty shabby and my doctor had me fitted with one that is a combination of neoprene rubber, Velcro and steel hinges. The steel hinges not only provide support but should you fall the steel hinges will only bend so far as to keep your knee from buckling completely under you like what has happened to me a few times. More and more players with injuries are using them and can see how it could get a player back in action, but I can also see how a tackler might get a finger caught in there so it is best to make sure the pants cover the hinges to prevent that.

There used to be a coach in the area who was always butting heads with officials and he would start playing head games right from the start. He would start trying to press your buttons as soon as you would meet him. The referee would ask him if his players were all properly equipped and he would usually reply with, "They better be," or "I sure hope so!" He would give you anything but a definite yes or no. Usually it was like this all game long and when he ran into trouble and left town I didn't shed a tear for him. And that is unfortunate because most coaches are pretty good guys but there are exceptions.

In all my years, though I have had to make a lot of decisions on equipment, the most memorable moment did not revolve around what a player had but more what he didn't have, LEGS! There was a school that had a young man who was a double amputee and wanted to play football. I had heard about him from other officials and I think there was an article in the paper about it. In any event, the coach wanted to see if any of us had any concerns because earlier in the season there was a question since the rule book says that all players have to wear shoes. I thought to myself, "Give me a break!" There used to be a couple of officials I could envision making a stink over just such an issue. My take was that there were a lot of people, not to mention the player himself, who had to work just to get this kid the opportunity to play and I was not going to stand in their way. It turned out that there were doctors, athletic directors, school administrators and coaches; just to name a few who worked behind the scenes to give him the chance to get out there on the field. Besides, with two good legs I wasn't much of a football player and I was willing to bet this young man was probably better than me despite his handicap.

Not long after the game began did he come out onto the field propelling himself with his arms not too unlike one would when on crutches, just without the crutches. He would line up on defense opposite the center and as soon as the ball was snapped he would sort of propel himself forward and submarine the center or guard, usually clogging up the middle of the offensive line. Because he was so low he was nearly impossible to block. He had to have incredible upper body strength and I just had to marvel at his courage. It's funny, to this day I can't recall the outcome of that game, only the sight of that player coming off the ball and taking out the legs of one or two offensive lineman so that if the offense ran a play in that direction they would have to either go over or around them. After each play he was in, he would leave the field or return to the huddle grinning from ear to ear. He was the winner that night.

Once the coach verifies that his players are properly equipped we usually ask if they have any special plays. The reason for that is most teams have a trick play or two and that is just fine. These coaches have these plays saved for special occasions when they can catch the opposition off guard in hopes of pulling off a long gain or even score. Some of these plays may be disguised to look like one type of play and turn into another.

My old high school had a play where the QB dropped back to pass and the fullback would be lined up, supposedly prepared to block for him. As the QB dropped back past him, he would slip the ball to him just under his armpit between the rib cage and his right elbow. If the quarterback had long enough arms and was quick enough this could be done undetected with the rushing linemen zooming past the fullback after the fleeing quarterback. By the time it was discovered the quarterback didn't have the ball, hopefully the fullback would be considerably further down the field. On just this type of play, if the quarterback is a good enough actor the defenders may drag him down, thinking he still has the ball. If he is a real good actor he just may fool the official into thinking he still has the ball and blow the whistle thinking he is down, ruining the play.

This is the reason we ask for any trick plays and most of your better teams play pretty much straight-up football with an occasional flea flicker or two. It is usually the programs that are struggling that feel the need to resort to gadget plays of trickery. It seems though, that if a team has difficulty mastering the basic fundamentals of blocking, tackling they have little success with the complicated stuff.

So if you go up to one coach and he has few trick plays and you go up to the next and he has three pages you kind of get to thinking it might be a long night and you would probably be right.

When we meet the coaches, Roger gives the coach a little card with the names of all the crew members and usually points out the name of the official on his sideline so, as he puts it, "You can yell at him in person."

These two pre-game procedures crossed paths one night down in Gila Bend. You may be wondering where you heard of Gila Bend and if you watch the evening news and they mention the nation's hottest temperature it frequently is there. One night we went there and met the visiting coach. While we made small talk, it turned out he was originally from some place in New York state, not far from where Roger once lived. Next thing I knew they were exchanging Empire State memories like old pals, which was a good thing. So right about then the coach told him he had a little special item he had been working on. It seems that on a short yardage situation, he had his offensive linemen getting down into their three point stance and just as they were almost set they SLOWLY raised up in a sort of shift, presumably to cause the defense to jump offside. He even went as far as to demonstrate, and we told him if they moved slowly like he said there should be no problem. But if they jumped up as it says in the rules, "simulating action at the snap," it would result in a foul.

The game began and the visiting team pretty much had its way, and Roger and the coach were getting along just fine. He came out on the field during a couple time-outs and he was in a good mood and even at the half it was, "Roger, how is it going?... Roger, is there any problems with my kids?... Roger, do you see anything I need to be concerned about?"

The second half got going and they still were beating up on Gila Bend, and sure as hell the visitors got into a short yardage situation. During a time-out the coach came out and after the time-out as he exited the field he told Roger he was going to try his pet play. His linemen got down into their stance and all of a sudden jumped up faster than a Sunbeam toaster. The defense jumped across the line and everyone who had a yellow hankie tossed one on the field. Well, the visiting coach came all unglued, yelling, "Roger, I told you we were going to do that!" The official who worked his sideline tried to explain that if they pulled up suddenly it was a foul. He was having none of that and the rest of the game Roger could do no right. From then it was, "Roger, they are holding... Roger, that was a clip... Roger, that was a late hit!" It went on like that the rest of the game and even though the visiting team won handily that one play ruined his entire night. Roger and the coach might be from the same town, but New York state loyalty aside, Roger and his crew ruined his highlight reel. Roger was now a horse's ass.

Each crew chief has a pre-game conference to one degree or another. Some prefer to have an intense pre-game covering the rules, mechanics and special circumstances. Roger prefers to meet with the crew members prior to the season and go over essentially the same subjects in depth. Prior to each game we touch on these subjects briefly; the only exception is if we have a substitute that we may have not worked with before or there is some issue(s) surrounding the contest he wants to cover in detail. We usually can tell when there is just such an occasion because Roger will tell us to show up about forty-five minutes earlier than we usually do. That means be prepared because he has some important items we need to cover and wants all of us on the same page. I may be prejudiced but I feel that we are prepared just as well as any crew, but we have done our share of pressure cooker type games and it is on those occasions that our crew chief gets us prepared for those games as good as any. He is not overbearing but will not tolerate any interruptions or horseshit when he is conducting his pre-games and we all feel that is just fine.

Our association adopted a program long ago where Observers are utilized to evaluate officials for their performance with respect to allegedly mechanics only. Such examples are:

    Positioning on running, passing and kicking plays
    Hand signals
    Whistle use

Communications with players and coaches
Teamwork
Procedures during time-outs, measurements, between quarters
Appearance and physical fitness

In theory it is a good idea, the objective being to use retired officials or ones that have a bye week. The process was supposed to be objective and personalities were not supposed to matter or at least this was how the program was laid out for the working officials. One such individual ran a city park sports league and if you didn't want to work games in his league you went straight to the top of his shit list so you could count on him giving a lousy evaluation if he came to one of your games. There were a few others that for one reason or another seldom got a post-season playoff game and now seemed to use this opportunity to see to it that others didn't get one either. Secretly, they were referred to as the "Casper Crew." This was because they were big fat loudmouths that bore striking resemblance to the character Casper Gutman played by Sidney Greenstreet in the Maltese Falcon.

Well, it didn't take long for word to get around that if one of the Casper Crew showed up at your game on a Friday night be prepared to get ripped unless you kissed their behind or were one of their buddies. So now here was our crew one week and Roger called us during the week telling us to be early. It turned out the two schools that were playing that night had had a few fights and there were gang problems on both campuses. These two schools were backyard rivals so there were a number of things Roger wanted to cover prior to the game.

As usual Roger was concerned about on-field extra curricular activities and was in the process of going over what he wanted each of us to do to keep order, when in comes Mr. City Parks to our dressing room as we were just about to take the field. We were really focused and couldn't wait to get out there and get things started when this Observer wanted to go over what he expected to watch us for. At the time we could care less since there was a pressure cooker game ahead of us and I think he took exception to this since he was used to other crews kissing his ass to get a good evaluation and liked the attention.

The first half was tense and some of the kids were caught up in the emotion of the game and there was a lot of pushing and shoving along with a lot of vulgar name calling. After warnings to the teams the chipping did not let up. We had to toss a few unsportsmanlike fouls out there and once it became clear we were not going to tolerate this type of behavior both teams settled down and played football. Oh, there were a few lapses of discipline, but for the most part it was kept clean. At halftime we went in and were ready to discuss what, if anything we could have done differently in the first half to have avoided the unsportsmanlike fouls and what plans we had for the remainder of the game to keep order.

Now despite what some people may think, we as officials extract some sort of thrill out of dinging a player or coach for an unsportsmanlike foul and for most officials it is just the opposite. A good official looks upon it as a failure on their part in keeping order since we try to take a proactive approach, preferring to talk to the players and point out that what we call "chippy" behavior is not a part of the game rather than throw flags and toss people out from the game.

So anyway we were having a pretty detailed discussion when in comes the Observer who proceeded to interrupt us to tell us how he would have handled the game thus far. This type of intrusion serves no purpose other than to disrupt the meeting and has absolutely nothing to do with mechanics which was the purpose of the Observer program.

The second half went just about how the first half ended with intense but clean football. Towards the end one team began to pull ahead by a large margin and the team getting whipped began to feel the frustration and the quality of play suffered and all they wanted to do was pick fights. There were a few times we had to step between players after plays to get them to go to their respective huddles. It is during times like these that officiating can be very stressful and exhausting. But, when a contest such as this is over and as you are walking off the field and see both teams shaking hands in the middle of the field, it gives you a tremendous feeling of satisfaction that despite the intensity of the rivalry and heated emotions the game did not get out of control and officiating did not enter into the equation. Leaving the field some of the school administrators stopped to thank us for the job we did.

Back in the dressing room there sat the Casper Crew member waiting to tell us what he observed. You know I did not think it was possible to spend over two hours doing a football game and not do one single thing correctly. At least that was the impression we got since he ripped each and every member of the crew to shreds and I wondered if he saw the same game we had just done. After a while we just tuned him out because we were exhausted and just wanted to shower and go for pizza. Again, the subjects he was ripping us on had nothing to do with mechanics and focused on our selection of penalty calls and judgments. Afterwards we told Roger that we didn't appreciate this guy's interruptions and how he strayed from the true purpose of the Observer program. Later the next week Roger got the copies of the evaluation in the mail and sure as shit we were downgraded in every category and was he ever pissed off.

At the time Roger and I were on the Board of Directors of the local Football Official's Association and the Board had been having an ongoing duel with the Commissioner of Officials and his aide the Commissioner of Observers over inconsistencies between what the Casper Crews were supposed to rate officials on (mechanics) and what they were actually rating officials on (popularity, judgment). At the time, call it an amazing coincidence, but it seemed that just about every crew chief who was on the Board that had a member of the Casper Crew evaluate one of their games got an unfavorable evaluation later the next week.

A week or so later we were assigned another pressure cooker game and we got to the school, and when we went into the locker room there sat the same guy that ripped us two weeks before with a Cheshire Cat grin on his kisser. He did not have it long because Roger told him he could get his fat ass out of our dressing room. He also told him not to come in at halftime or after the game. Since he need not tell us about our performance since he was forbidden from bugging us after the game, he could send his lousy evaluation to Roger's post office box next week. Not only did he tell off this guy in front of the whole crew, he made sure the four man chain crew, who were also football officials, were present, thereby assuring that word would spread like wildfire among officiating circles. Roger got free pizza and beer that night following the game. I didn't figure we would get a playoff game that year but a few weeks later while doing a Pop Warner game one Saturday morning a couple guys came up to me between games and asked if it was true Roger tossed one of the Casper Crew from our pre-game. I told them it was indeed true and they remarked that that sort of incident should occur more often. Roger was a hero of sorts.

Every so often when I would arrive for a contest I would find out that one or more of my crew members had arrived prior to me, which made it easier for the "guy with the key" to direct me to the proper area. On one night, oh my gosh, we got a playoff game and it was at Chandler High School about two miles from my house. It was a Class A playoff game and they play on a field eighty yards long and forty yards wide. There was another game at that site just before ours and the game was just completed when I arrived and the crew from that game was in there showering after the game. I was chatting with them when the game administrator came in and informed me that through a glitch they marked the field so that the field they used for the previous game and would be used for our game was one hundred yards long but forty yards wide and the AIA had said that it was okay. I had a momentary flashback and just blurted out, "It will be like playing touch football on my street in Youngstown, Ohio, from telephone pole to telephone pole."

At that point one of the guys from the previous crew asked, "Are you from Youngstown?" and when I told him I was, he informed me he was from Youngstown as well and had graduated from Rayen High School where Ron Demesko, an old family friend had taught.

Now once you get to the contest there is the expectation of privacy and again most schools due a good job assuring the officials can dress and shower in peace, but from time to time there are slip-ups.

The majority of the time the games I have done are in central or northeast Phoenix. Since I live in Mesa I usually have to drive the farthest. That means having to negotiate the East Valley freeways during rush hour so I leave early and usually am the first to arrive. This way I take my good old time getting dressed. I usually partially dress in gym shorts, T-shirt and socks. If I am early enough I may shoot the breeze with coaches, athletic directors, etc., eat a protein bar and Gatorade and just generally relax.

So one school put us in an office that served as the coach's office for the girl's locker room. The office was surrounded on three sides by brick walls with the fourth wall just from the floor to about three or four feet high. From there it was glass from the top of the wall to the ceiling which faced the girl's locker room, evidently to monitor activity by the coaches. This one night we had a substitute official and the rest of the guys filtered in one by one, but the sub was a late arrival. We were all sitting around discussing the records of the two schools scheduled that night and going over pre-game preparations when Frank walked in as the rest of us were just about all dressed. He hurriedly began to dress and was butt naked from the waist down, just about ready to pull his knickers up with his back turned, his behind facing the glass. All of a sudden the door to the locker room flew open and about six cheerleaders came bouncing in and through the glass were face to face with Frank's butt. Each did an abrupt about face and bounced out the locker room, several of them shrieking to high heaven.

The whole thing was over in a few seconds and Frank had no idea what happened. We told him what occurred while his back was to the window. He was worried about taking the field lest the cheerleaders recognize him and all he could envision was snickers and giggles from the teenage girls. I told him he could feel safe since the only features they could possibly recall was that the culprit had one brown eye and a big nose.

You have arrived at the game, had the pre-game conference, and gotten dressed. Once you are dressed you might want to look in a mirror and make sure you look professional. You don't have to look like you belong on the cover of *Referee Magazine*, but look neat and clean.

Early on our old crew chief Elmer had a white hat that over the years had stains and looked more yellow than white. The brim was crooked and just looked like hell. We actually had a game that was close to town and there was a chance that there might be someone in attendance we might actually know and we tried to encourage him to get a new hat and he agreed he would get a new white hat by then.

Looking back on it we should have just kicked in a few bucks apiece and bought him a new hat. But for whatever reason we didn't. As the game day arrived we showed up at the school and were getting dressed when Elmer broke out his new hat. It seemed his daughter gave it to him as a present or something like that. All I can say is his daughter has a sense of humor. The cap was new all right and it was white, well mostly white. On the front of the cap was the name of some construction company and a picture of a bulldozer all printed in bright red. The rest of us thought it was a joke but Elmer insisted it was not and he had every intention of wearing it during the game. Besides, he'd already destroyed the other cap. All we could do was pray that no one saw us who was in a position to send us in the future to game sites as far removed from the Phoenix area as humanly possible.

After the game we pleaded with him to at least cover the red bulldozer and the printing with white fabric. As we pointed out how ridiculous it looked, he agreed to cover it up, reluctantly.

The next week he showed up and assured us he covered the printing and the bulldozer. When he pulled it out of his bag it turns out he took some white enamel and looked like he slathered it on with a trowel. When the paint hardened it had a glossy finish that reflected the light like a hard hat.

It was not long after that when the rest of us had a meeting with Roger and decided that maybe our crew needed a new crew chief.

All dressed up and got some place to go? If you have not found him yet you got to go locate another person. That is the guy or gal with the checks. Sometimes it is the guy with the key, more often than not it isn't.

Schools will pay by check or as in the case of the Glendale School District they pay in cash, which is great since a number of schools in that district are in close proximity to *Tommy's*, one of our favorite places to go for pizza and wings. I don't know why but it seems that after a Friday night game in the Glendale district we seem to eat more pizza and wings and the beer and soda taste a little better. I'm sure the waitress doesn't mind either because we are all bigger tippers on those nights. Friday is karaoke night at Tommy's as well and Hank's singing always seems to sound better after a game at a Glendale School District high school than anywhere else. Like I've said, we are not in it for the money.

Speaking of money there are valuables. In the more than twenty years I've never had a problem with valuables, however, I remember an old saying, "If you can't afford to lose it, leave it at home!" I remember hearing about an incident some years ago when there was a playoff game in Tucson and someone broke into the official's dressing room and removed some valuables, but they were caught. I remember a game once when I was bringing the visiting team's captains out for the opening coin toss and one young man was visibly shaken. I dismissed it as pre-game jitters but one of his teammates said that their lockers were broken into. The shaken young man had a $5,000 necklace stolen. My first reaction was what was a high school student doing with a necklace that expensive and second what was he doing bringing it to a Friday night football game? To my knowledge it was never recovered.

Mark, our back judge has the right idea. He grew up in inner city Chicago. As a youth he would walk part of the way to Comiskey Park, home of the White Sox. He said that just walking down the street someone would confront you and try to kick your ass and take your money. That in mind, he would keep his wallet in his sock and does so to this day and that includes game nights.

CHAPTER VI

TAKING THE FIELD

You're all dressed and ready to go so the crew takes the field. The rule of thumb is that you should get out there at least thirty minutes before the scheduled kickoff. Actually, rules mandate that the officials take over official control of the contest at that time.

In some parts of the country the clock operator is an official, too. In Arizona the clock operator can be just about anybody so for that reason one crew member meets with the clock operator in person. You want to find out if they have ever done this before or if the clock is working properly and that sort of thing. It is not just a matter of turning the clock off and on, it's knowing when to run the clock and when not to. One game we had a person who was supposedly an experienced clock operator which he was but for basketball. As a result every time he heard a whistle blow he would stop the clock. After the first quarter took forever we had a little talk with him and things moved a little better. There have been extreme cases where we have had to fire the clock operator and keep the time on the field.

St. Mary's High School is a little inner city Catholic school in downtown Phoenix that plays its JV games across the street in Monterey Park. They don't have a scoreboard so they keep the time on the field and they have a little old guy that has done it for years. This guy is terrific. He is usually there well before the game starts and comes up to the officiating crew and introduces himself although most crews have worked with this fellow in the past.

When the game starts he moves up and down the sidelines as the game moves, giving the crew frequent reminders of how much time is remaining in the quarter. If the game is a blowout he shaves off a few seconds here and there to move the game along a bit. He has been there so long that Dave Garcia who is now a veteran football official attended St. Mary's and recalls this man running the clock when he was in high school over twenty years ago.

Another thing about little St. Mary's is that even though it is a small inner city school, they fight to stay in the 5-A division, the state's largest division and they usually are one of the toughest. They have a huge following and at some of their JV games there will be bigger crowds than at some high school varsity games. When you arrive at Monterey Park to do one of these games and take the field, you notice something is missing besides a scoreboard, one of the goal posts. Well it really isn't missing so much, just that it is unusual that it abuts a residential neighborhood. An extra point try could easily knock out a window, so the goal post at the west end of the field is the only one you can use, which means that if a team scores at the east end of the field and wants to try a kick for the extra point, everybody has to run down to the other end of the field, do the extra point and turn the teams around for the ensuing kickoff. One coach made us run all the way down to the other end of the field for the try only to fake it and run for it. This was all while up by thirty points late in the game.

Behind the goal post at the west end of the field is a tall palm tree that at first glance looks like coconuts up in the branches. Wrong! I was looking up there one night and noticed that there were about a half dozen footballs stuck in there. I asked one of the coaches about it and he told me that during practice and JV games balls kicked too high get stuck in the palm fronds. Once or twice a year a few of the firemen from the Phoenix Fire Station around the corner come by with their ladder truck and extricate the imprisoned footballs.

So now both teams are usually on the field when you first walk out there and someone from the home team will meet you and give you the game ball. Since I handle the ball in just about every play as the umpire, they automatically give it to me. As long as it is shaped like a football and has air in it that is good enough for me. I have heard of umpires that carry tire gauges with them to measure how much air is in the ball since the rule book does say that the ball has to have between twelve and a half to thirteen and a half pounds of air pressure. Another told me that he just bites down on the end of the ball and if it feels too soft then he has them put more air in it. I think if my fellow crew members saw me whip out a tire gauge or taking a bite out of a game ball they would have a net thrown over me so fast it would make my head spin.

With game ball in hand you go visit the other team and while doing so present them with the game ball to inspect. The rules say that a team may use any legal ball of its choice; it does not have to use the game ball provided by the home team if they choose not to. However, just about all home schools like to put their best foot forward and the game ball that they give you is usually a brand new one of the best quality. Now you go to the visiting team and they will take a look at it and usually have the starting quarterback try a snap or two with it. More than half the time he will prefer to use their own ball when they are on offense. Then they will go and get the ball and what do you know, it is the same damn ball. Same brand, same condition and same air pressure. You could hold them next to each other and not tell them apart. So now you have to go and find someone who will act as the ball boy. More often than not it is a player who is injured and not suited up and we try to tell him to keep up with us and to exchange the ball after a change in possession. You know, pay attention to what is happening on the field, which means that each time you need to change game balls he is fifty yards up the field bullshitting with cheerleaders or a couple of teammates. Good ball boys help make the game flow a lot smoother.

You like to find out if there are any special events that will take place before the game. For homecoming or seniors' night for example they may bring out the parents and players and introduce them one by one. These events can be time-consuming but I know how important it can be for the players. When I was in school my mother used to come to the homecoming since my father had already died and even though she didn't know much about football and chances of me playing were between slim and none it was still important to me. I'm sure the same goes for today's kids.

You also like to know about special events to make sure they don't inadvertently affect the playing conditions. In Apache Junction one night it was homecoming and one of the local television stations had a popular personality that was a helicopter traffic commentator. They thought it would be a novel idea for him to fly his chopper to mid-field and drop off the homecoming queen along with the game ball. After doing so he lifted off to a standing ovation from the home crowd at which he dipped the helicopter rotors in kind of an airborne salute, thus blowing over all the yard line and end zone markings on the home side of the field. Not to be out done, the fans on the visiting side of the field began to whoop and holler at which point he turned the helicopter around and did a similar salute, blowing down all the markings on the opposite side of the field.

Some of the results of these events are not so clearly visible. One school up in the high country has a team of riders on horseback parade out on the field prior to the National Anthem. We did a game up there one year and not too long after it began Scott Williams who was the line judge that night was running up the field trailing a play when somewhere between the sideline and the hash marks stepped in a big pile of horseshit. That I am sure is not covered in the official's manual.

Home team game administration has a lot to do, I'll give you that, but, it just seems that a lot of thought is not given to the chain and chain crew. It is at times like this I have all the sympathy in the world for the head linesman since the burden of working with them falls squarely on his shoulders.

First thing they do is unravel the chains, stretch them out and compare them to the field markings to see if they are actually ten yards long. Along about this time it is a good idea to check the condition of the chains themselves. Besides the chains there is a metal pole with numbers attached to indicate what down it is. This device is called "The Box." The newer ones consist of a series of slats kind of like a set of Venetian blinds and a lever on one side. A mere flick of the lever and the slats change to form the numbers one through four. Some of the older Boxes have four thin metal sheets with two holes drilled on the top and held together with metal rings. To change the down all you need to do is flip the numbers to indicate the correct down number. It is not unusual to find that over the years the metal rings can become worn and could break apart and the whole contraption fall apart right in the middle of the game. This is also true for the metal sheets. The ring holes in the top can become worn like the holes in a sheet of notebook paper in a three ring binder. Probably the term "The Box" comes from what they used to use at my old high school. For our freshman and JV games we had a metal rod about six feet long. About two-thirds of the way up they had affixed a red wooden box about a foot square. On the panels on each side of the box there were painted in white the numbers one through four. I've never seen another one like it since, although I've seen plenty on old football films. The only problem was that unless you were able to see the side of the box that faced the field you couldn't tell what down it was. The newer ones you can see what down it is from just about anywhere on the field. Of course that assumes your chain crew is on the same page as the officials and have the correct down number displayed. For that reason all five of us have wrist bands that serve as down indicators and we are constantly reminding one another of what down it is because it is a major mess up to give a team an extra down or to shortchange them of one.

    Chain crew members have a tendency to daydream from time to time and may not flip the down marker when told to do so. Early in my career I worked as a line judge a lot and a lot of the chain crews I had were reluctant participants to say the least. One game I looked to the sideline to tell the kid working the down box what down it was only to find him hunched over with the down box straddling his knee and he was strumming it like a guitar and shaking his hips like Elvis Presley.

There have been times when they have to ask people in the stands to volunteer to serve as chain crew members. Many do so reluctantly. I have been at games where one or two chain crew members just simply left, obviously having something better to do. One school had an all girl chain crew that spent most of their evening chatting up the players.

One of my buddies told me of a game he did one time where the school was on break and the only chain crew members they could rustle up were four foreign exchange students from China who spoke little English.

Remember little St. Mary's? The first time I did one of their varsity games I thought the Association made a mistake and assigned two crews to do the game because as soon as I took the field I saw four other guys dressed exactly like me. It turns out that they were the chain crew, a group of St. Mary's faithful that work each home game they play at Phoenix College. Just like the clock operator at the JV games, the same guys have done it every home game and have done it for what seems like forever. I think they buy and maintain their own uniforms and I bet they don't get paid a dime. They keep right up with the game, don't move until told to do so and pay close attention to what is happening out on the field. Oh, once in a while they may slip a little signal to the coach how far the line to gain may be after a close play, but what of it?

The ideal chain crew is the rookie officials who have to fulfill chain crew requirements before they can get moved up the ladder. Unfortunately, in recent years the number of new officials coming into the state is dwindling so the chain crews consisting of actual officials are few and far between.

Before the game and during halftime we usually strike up a conversation with the chain crew members and may tell them what they could do to move things along. During one such break at a JV game at Arcadia the chain crew came up to us and we talked with them and Roger noticed that one of the kids on the chain crew was huge. This kid had to have been over 250 pounds and he looked to be about only fourteen years old. So he asked him how come he wasn't playing and he said he was on the team but was injured and assured us he was going to go out for football again next season. About that time one of the other kids on the chain crew piped up, "I'm going out for football, too!" Well this kid could not have weighed more than a hundred pounds soaking wet, so I said to him that I hoped he put on a few more pounds before doing so and he said, "Why, I weigh over 160 pounds." I told him he was out of his mind and that if he weighed that much I was Abraham Lincoln. So all four of us and the rest of the chain crew laughed at him and he adamantly said, "I can prove it, it says so on my birth certificate!" At that point everyone cracked up and the kid stomped off, adamantly pleading his case to everyone in ear shot.

While you are out on the field before a game, a coach or assistant may walk up to you and ask about a particular rule and usually as a result of a call in a previous game. Now he may describe a play and even demonstrate it for you and ask your opinion. Now just like Roger's buddy from New York, what he may be telling you might not be what actually occurred on the play. I don't say whether another official made a good or bad call. I let them have their say and just try to explain the rule to them and leave it go at that. But sometimes these inquiries can be kind of interesting. Many years ago there was a guy locally who was somewhat of a legend. Not that he was that great an official but because of his view of the federal government which he shared with anyone who would listen. This guy who I'll call "Little" did not believe in taxes to the extent that he did not have a driver's license because he felt the fee for the license was a form of taxation. Well it seems that Little was a stickler for equipment and he would find some little quirk and just focus on that. Since Little had no driver's license someone had to drive him to the games. Little had dropped out of sight and we had not seen him at any of the rules meetings or kickoff meetings. We didn't see him at any of the Pop Warner games or anything and we had heard that he was living up near Las Vegas but no one ever confirmed that.

It had to have been about a dozen years later and we were doing a game here in town and the visiting team was from the Kingman/Lake Havasu area which is on the way to Vegas. One of the assistant coaches comes up to us before the game and starts griping about the crew that did their game the week before at their school. He tells us that the crew was late for the game because they had to pick up the crew chief and it put them off schedule. Soon after they get there he noticed they had cleats on that didn't exactly meet the specifications of the rule book (I think they were ceramic of something) and made the kids change their shoes. It turns out Little is alive and well in northwest Arizona.

Once you take the field there is as they say no turning back. That meaning once you're there you are pretty much committed to working the contest, a concept that is clung to dearly by the older officials. To coin a phrase once uttered by one of the most veteran officials, the only reason to miss an assigned contest is "if you are in a pine box carried by six of your friends."

On a Thursday afternoon one such official was scheduled to work a freshman game at Brophy Prep, a private school in central Phoenix. Paul who had to have been in his seventies and had lost more than a step or two showed up as scheduled looking a little pale. Paul also seemed a little more lethargic than usual and as he joined the rest of the crew he announced that the boys may have to carry him tonight since he was not feeling like his good old self. So everyone figured Paul was coming down with the flu or something and they inquired as to what was ailing him out of genuine concern since Paul was a nice guy and colorful as well. Paul told them he had just had prostate surgery and was still feeling a bit weak. They told him all he had to do was call one of them and they would have found a last-minute replacement. Well, Paul told them there wasn't enough time as the surgery was this morning. So Paul wasn't in a pine box but he was at Brophy, at least in body. Everyone else did a little more than usual and Paul gutted it out. Paul didn't take himself too seriously but took his assignments very seriously.

At some point the referee and umpire walked the field. To some it may have looked like we were just ambling about aimlessly. We looked for exposed sprinkler heads which we found a lot of. That is resolved by tossing a shovel of dirt over it. Many have heard the story of how Mickey Mantle's career was affected after he stepped into one of those back in the '50s.

We usually checked the field markings to see if the lines were straight. One night the athletic director came up to us as we were doing just that. This was a small rural school district that was financially strapped. So the AD expressed his concern over the quality of the field markings and informed us, "I was out here earlier in the day and did the best I could with a bag of flour and a soup can." We assured him the lines were just fine and he did a masterful job.

Some things just can't be changed. Some older schools it seems were just built into the available landscape and athletic facilities just had to be made to fit. One such case was the old football stadium at Wickenburg about forty-five miles northwest of Phoenix. It seems that the running track cuts through the northeast corner of the back of the end zone. They used to have a traffic cone up against the fence and I guess if a receiver caught a pass up against that fence it was considered in play, kind of like arena football.

As you walk the field you can't help but note the condition of the field and the facilities, good and bad. One of the newer high schools in northeast Scottsdale has a campus the size of a small college. They have the officials dress in the theatrical dressing room, kind of what you would find in a Broadway theatre.

But one facility that I used to enjoy doing a game at was the old Phoenix Indian School. Partly because the field was cut like a putting green and one year we did a playoff game there and the field was marked with the individual yard markings like a college field. The only fault I could find in it was the field did not have a crown like most do but was actually concave. But since it rains so seldom in the valley it is hardly a concern. The first time I did a game there I had seen the field from another nearby campus.

Central High in Phoenix has its football field face 7th Street. It is interesting since the school faces Central Avenue a good half mile away. That is one of the schools that at halftime if you try to walk to your dressing room you may as well turn around and start back because the intermission is half over. So when at Central the old Indian High field is about a hundred yards to the southeast of theirs. You can see one from the other.

So I got a playoff game there one year and the school itself was pretty old and dilapidated having been built I think in the 1800s. We got dressed and headed out to the field and there was a playing surface that was the nicest I had ever been on. Like I said the field was cut like a golf course and the turf was as soft as could be. This was in the final days of Phoenix Indian's existence as the land was sold and the school closed. The Indian's football teams were not very competitive and some of the regular season games I did there afterward were pretty lopsided and the all Native American student body did not lose their enthusiasm. Although the campus has long since been closed down and earmarked for other uses, I can't help when I have occasion to drive by the intersection of 3rd Street and Indian School Road but recall the old Phoenix Indian School. Here was a site early in my career where I did my first playoff game on the meticulous turf on that old gridiron. I think the local association made a good decision in those days to use the school as a neutral site for the 1-A playoff games before the school was razed and I was thankful for the opportunity to work a game there.

You know that once you take the field the game is going to get started sooner or later and there are a few things you have to get out of the way beforehand.

Most teams go into the locker rooms before the game and a few minutes before kickoff try to make a grand entrance with their band playing some sort of fight song and those in attendance getting worked into frenzy as the players sprint onto the field. The home team is usually the last of the two to enter the stadium and the home team tries to make their entrance louder and more spirited that their visiting counterparts. So as not to be outdone some schools will try various forms of showmanship to accomplish that goal. I have seen pyrotechnic salutes and scoreboards that have flashing lights and sirens. One of the copper mining towns that are situated on the side of a mountain allows spectators to park their pickup trucks along a slag pile that overlooks the high school football field for one dollar a truckload. Back in the mid '80s I did a game there for the one and only time I visited this community.

The folks that took advantage of this service I think do so because they can take items up on the slag heap to watch the game with that they cannot ordinarily take into a regular high school stadium. Those items I think include alcoholic beverages and rifles. Now I may be wrong about the libations but I'm pretty sure on the firearms because when the home team ran onto the field the hillside erupted into gunfire aimed skyward. Now there are some who may claim that what I actually heard were firecrackers but having been raised and served as an inner city policeman in Youngstown, Ohio (some refer to it as Murdertown, USA), I'm pretty sure I know the sound of gunfire when I hear it. Not that I'm complaining at all, in fact it made me kind of home sick. Besides, they were aimed up into the air. Just as a precaution I tried be extra sharp that night.

One school tried to make the start of one of their homecoming games extra special so they had a couple hundred helium inflated balloons collected under a large plastic drop cloth. At the precise moment the drop cloth would be pulled off releasing the balloons into the night sky in a hundred different directions. But as the gridders entered the field and the cover pulled back for some reason the balloons did not disperse as they arose from the field. Instead they all stuck together in one large oval-shaped, red and blue mass that resembled a small blimp and drifted up and away into the night.

Again, having spent most of my adult life in a smoke- and pollution-filled blue collar city I never really got into getting all lathered up over sunrises and sunsets because half the rime I didn't get a good look at them. Now one of the things I like about the crew I referee with is that we all can have a good time at each of the other's expense. If you can't handle a lot of good-natured ribbing this is one group of guys you might want to steer clear of. So you can imagine how I felt one night as the start of a game approached and there we all were assembled at midfield. Roger and Scott Williams looked to the western sky like they were in a trance. I walked up to the two of them figuring maybe they dropped some acid and ask them what the hell was the big attraction, and Scott said that he and Roger were "admiring the beautiful sunset!"

In Arizona they don't turn the clocks ahead for Daylight Savings Time so the opportunities for viewing pre-game sunsets are limited to the first week or two of the season. But, from that day forward if I ever catch the two of them even glancing to the west I'll usually go up to them and say something like, "The rest of us can get the game started without you two guys if you want to go up in the stands and hold hands while the sun goes down."

It was at one time the rules for blocking were that the blocker had to keep his hands in and the block be thrown using the forearm and the shoulder, primarily the shoulder. The hands could be closed or cupped with the palms facing inward and the elbows could be inside or outside the frame of the body extended not more than forty-five degrees from the body. Then the open-hand blocking technique was adopted and the blocker's hands could be extended beyond the elbow with contact between the shoulders at or below the opponent's numbers. Occasionally the hands of the blocker get caught under the shoulder pads of the opponent, sometimes by accident and sometimes on purpose. Right after this change we had a game in which the visiting team was coached by a guy who in his playing days was a Phoenix Union High School legend. As a coach he had a team that had a tough time of things talent-wise and discipline-wise as well.

He came up to us as we were walking the field and told us that he and his assistants had watched film of the opponent and number 77 on offense sure looked to be holding a lot. We assured him we would watch for it. He went on to tell us that he felt that every time he went "north of the river," his team seemed to get the short end of the stick. He felt that his team was being singled out because they were from a depressed area or at least it seemed like that. You know no matter how hard you try you cannot placate some people and it is something you just have to live with. But now with video cameras everywhere I wish I could have put a camera on a guy like this just to play it back for him later in life so they can see what a fool they made of themselves just for the sake of a high school football game.

So the night in question all five of us watch this kid and I think we may have caught him once or twice but for the most part you could have played the film back for a clinic on what a good blocking technique truly was. The fact of the matter was that this number 77 was just dominant. He didn't need to cheat; he accomplished his goal by just good hard football. Well, the visiting coach, what basically amounted to good blocking technique to him equated to holding and he let us know about it on just about every play.

This was just after Roger started giving out crew members names to the coaches so they "can holler at us in person." The official on this coach's sideline was Bob Cripe, one of the most even-tempered people I have ever met. But not on this night because all we heard from that sideline besides "They're holding on every play!" was "Bobby Cripe, you're killing me!" The further behind his team got the more they were holding on every play and the more Bob Cripe got away with a capital crime. This is about the point where a coach acting like an asshole is observed by his players and they see him doing it and they think if the coach is doing it then it must be all right for them to do it. If there is little discipline to contend with they emulate their coach which in turn spills over into the stands and the spectators start in on us. There is no way you can shut everyone on the sideline up so you just have to tune it out and not get "rabbit ears."

When you are out there before a game you get approached by school administrators who may have concerns that we occasionally take back to the association to see if they want to look into it. One such concern I heard mentioned more than once was six or seven years ago, the powers that be came up with the idea to change to timing rule. It used to be that after a scrimmage kick, kickoff or change in possession, if the ball became dead in the field of play and there was no foul, the clock started once the ball was spotted and the referee signaled the ready-for-play.

The rule was changed and from that day forward the clock was started when the ball was snapped. If you had a game with a lot of kicks, a sloppy game with a lot of turnovers or a combination of both it would stretch out the time it took to play the game up to as much as a half hour to an hour. Along with a lot of other officials I didn't particularly care for this change, especially in lopsided contests where the frustration factor rises along with the score. One of the reasons that were given for the change was that is was for "fairness." The way it was explained to me was that especially on kicking plays there was confusion getting the special teams off the field and the respective offenses and defenses on the field in time for the play. This explanation didn't make any sense to me because once the play is over, no matter what the play, the ball is placed at the spot on the field where the next play will commence. The whistle is blown for the ready to play and the offense has twenty-five seconds to snap the ball regardless if the clock is running or not, so I could not see how that excuse could be made.

I figured no one asked me so what I thought didn't amount to a hill of beans. If it took a while longer to get the game over with so be it; the pizza would taste better and the beer a little colder. It's not as if I have anywhere to be at ten o'clock on a Friday night and I got paid the same no matter how long it took. Not long after the change in the rule, though, I had a conversation with more than one school administrator who had a different view on the subject.

A high school football game doesn't just happen. There are lots of people that are integral to a contest such as off-duty police for security, firefighter EMT's in case of illness or injury, and maintenance staff just to name a few. All these people are paid hourly and in the case of police and firefighters are on overtime status. Administrators concerned over the extended game times in paying these individuals and then multiply that times five or six home games and it was putting a strain on already tight school budgets. I didn't look at the change as a big deal until it was put to me in that light. As officials we tried to communicate that to the powers that be through our regional associations but there was never a change. I once read a publication that on a national level the rule change resulted in an average extended length of football contests to be a mere seven minutes. To that I have two things to say. First of all, whoever did that survey needed to follow me around for a season or two. Secondly, I hope that my wife never reads this or else how the hell can I come rolling in past midnight after a seven o'clock game and not have been unfaithful for years.

For years Roger was the area assigner for Pop Warner football and the luxury of that was that we could call him and tell him what free time we had on a Saturday and he would assign us games accordingly.

Myself and Scott liked to work the eight o'clock morning games at Central High before it got too hot. I lived around the corner at the time and it was a quick and easy twenty bucks.

The first week of the season Scott and I were awaiting the start of the game and this little fat kid about ten or eleven came walking up to us to see if we needed a ball boy, but we didn't so we basically told him thanks but no thanks. This kid was about as big around as he was tall and I was unsure if he would keep up even if we needed a ball boy. Each Saturday morning we would do an eight o'clock game at Central and there he would be just kind of hanging around. Seldom did we see him that he didn't have something in his hand to eat. He would be chowing down on concession stand goodies or munching orange slices that were supposed to be for the players or a bag of peanut butter and jelly sandwiches he brought from home. It didn't matter. There he would be waddling up to the field before those Pop Warner games one week after another. On the Saturday after Thanksgiving we were out there before our game and the little fat kid was nowhere to be seen. Our first thought was that he overdosed on stuffing but he surfaced a few years later which we'll get back to when we discuss halftime festivities, but for the longest time Scott and myself would wonder what happened to the "Ho Ho Kid."

Every once in a while just before a game there may be other officials we know in attendance and they may stop and say hello. If they are like me they keep their gym bag with their gear in their car just in case an official goes down with an injury and you need a last-minute substitute. In any case it's good to see old friends we don't see as often and see how they have been. One such official was Dave T. Dave had been a crew chief for years but once his sons were old enough to play football at McClintock High in Tempe he took a couple of seasons off so he could watch his sons play in JV and varsity games.

Not having him available for Fridays was a bummer because he was very professional and his crew was always sharp. His professional demeanor reflected well on all officials. He was very soft spoken and not a loudmouth and was just an all around good guy. So needless to say when doing a game at McClintock running into Dave T. was always a pleasant surprise and we would ask him to stop by at halftime if he saw anything that we might be doing that we could improve on or if he had any comments. Dave had been around for many years and had done all the big games so his input was always welcome. I think for a while there they were using Dave as an Observer which I thought was an excellent idea.

Just as there are guys like Dave T. who we are always happy to see, there are a few that might just as well stay in the stands because they make a real pain of themselves.

For a few years we had a man on our crew Tommy Vaughn who played about seven or eight seasons with the Detroit Lions from the late '60s until the mid '70s. I looked up his stats one day and he had a rather impressive amount of yardage on punt returns. Well Tommy has since retired from officiating because of a neck or back injury which is a shame because he was one of the funniest guys I had ever met. He had a terrific personality and was a real charmer who, as Scott Williams said more than once, "Tommy could sell ice cubes to an Eskimo."

I particularly liked when he told of when he was an assistant college football coach and he would get sent to some inner city school to recruit a player. Some of those schools resemble inner city jungles and were quite nasty. He would tell me how he would be worried some young thug was about to stick a knife in his ribs but he never let it show. He would tell of walking down the hall of one of these schools with a magazine rolled up in his fist and the meanest scowl he could manage. He said he would saunter down the hall, eyes straight ahead like the meanest son of a bitch there ever was and nobody would mess with him.

Well about that time there was one of the Observers who would show up on the sideline at one of our game using the fact that he was there to observe us as a pretext so he could just gush at the thought of rubbing elbows with a real NFL player. This guy would tell each of us what a horseshit job we were doing and then fawn all over our NFL veteran line judge.

So ridiculous this guy was, he came up to us and asked Roger and me, "What is that bullshit you guys are doing before each kickoff?"

That bullshit he was referring to was when there are four officials, prior to the kickoff the line judge is positioned on about the receiver's twenty or thirty yard line and the umpire is up around midfield with the kickers. Roger went to a referee's seminar in California once and they suggested flip flopping the umpire and the line judge on kickoffs. There are two reasons for this. First off, particularly in my case, most umpires are big and slow. After a score you have to get the ball and run all the way back up field for the ensuing kickoff. In a high-scoring contest this can be rough on my already bad knees. The second and most logical reason is that having the linesman and line judge up around midfield is great if a receiver breaks off a big run. The linesman and line judge usually have the best legs on the crew and can stay with the runner should he break off a long kick return. This saves a lot of wear and tear on the umpire and we have affectionately called this change "fat man's mechanics."

This is what the Observer was referring to on this night. He went on to say, "You better not let the Commissioner catch you guys doing that shit. He sees that shit and you guys will never do another game in this state!" Well, that really put the fear of God into us. That was over twelve years ago and we are still doing the fat man mechanics as is every other crew in the country since it has been adopted nationally. I like to think that just because you might be a pioneer you don't have to take yourself too seriously.

The game time was rapidly approaching and to get things going there's almost always the National Anthem. When I was in high school there was one year that money was real tight and there were no bands for most of the football games, but they just played a recording of the National Anthem before each game. Although having a band is more traditional, playing a tape or recording is sometimes better than having a poorly prepared band butcher the piece.

One year we were up in Payson, a city up in the mountains about seventy miles northeast of the valley. So there we were and it was getting close to game time but no band was to be found anywhere. Right about game time we saw the game administration setting up a microphone at midfield so I figured maybe the choir or something like that was going to set up and sing the National Anthem. Instead, they trotted out some kid with a trombone. They announced the beginning of the anthem and a color guard prepared to raise the flag and the kid broke out into a trombone solo version of the National Anthem. We figured somewhere Frances Scott Key was spinning in his grave because what was coming out of that horn had little resemblance to what he wrote that night. So horrible was the presentation we had to hide our faces behind our caps to conceal the laughter.

The National Anthem having been played, it was now time to get the captains out to the middle of the field for the coin toss. Now one thing I have always tried to remember is something a veteran official told me when my career was in its infancy. He always said that no matter how small the game or how little it may mean to the league standings, to those kids out there playing it is like the Super Bowl. I try to keep that in mind and if I get a chance to talk with them, treat them with respect. A lot of schools rotate their captains the start of each game to give as many players as possible the chance to share in the experience. A great idea mind you but you are dealing with kids and the prospect of being captain and all the pageantry of the coin toss can lead to confusion.

The winner of the coin toss has the choice of kicking, receiving, deciding which goal to defend or deferring their choice until the start of the second half. Coaches have been deferring the choice until the start of the second half, however that message sometimes gets lost with the player out in the middle of the field. Thinking the coach wants to receive at the start of the second half the winning captain may elect to kick off to start the game, thereby forfeiting any choice in the second half. There have been a couple times when the captain just froze up altogether. One night at South Mountain High the home team won the toss and after given his choice of kicking, receiving, defending a goal or deferring, merely said, "We want the rock!"

A while back we decided that when we had our pre-game meeting with the coaches we would ask them that if their captain wins the coin toss at the start of the game what would he like for the captain to say. This way if the kid becomes confused or freezes up entirely we can get it right After all it really doesn't hurt anything but help move the game along.

Now we officials are human and we goof up from time to time. One Saturday I was the referee for a Pop Warner game. Well, not used to being the referee I forgot to bring a coin for the toss so I was canvassing the rest of the crew members for a coin. I ended up using a penny for the coin toss but what are you going to do?

The coin toss is another difference between high school football and the games you see on TV on Sundays. On those big TV games they toss the coin into the air and it lands on a beautifully manicured turf with the smoothness of a billiard table. But, I have been on some high school football field where the grass is so high and thick or covered with mud so thick that if the coin lands just so, there is a good chance it will land sideways. Even worse, is the end of the season, when the fields are a mess of dust and dead grass clippings that if you drop a coin on the ground there is a good chance you'll never find it again. For that reason we always have the referee toss the ball into the air and catch it.

For the group of guys I work with even though the coin toss is completed the game is not ready to begin. All five of us meet in the middle of the field where as we do each game we remind one another the first one to throw a flag after the start of the second half has to buy the first round of beers afterward. If we are not loosened up by that point Roger brings out his University of Michigan key chain that when you press it plays "The Victors" the Michigan fight song. At that point we remind each other, "Don't fuck it up." At that point we break the huddle and go to our respective positions on the field.

CHAPTER VII

LET'S GET THE SHOW ON THE ROAD

Once the teams are set you have the referee at one end of the field and once everyone is set he blows the whistle at which point the kicking team has twenty-five seconds to kick the ball. Usually both benches are hollering, the cheerleaders and fans screaming and drums pounding loudly. Once the ball is kicked and goes beyond ten yards, it can be picked up by either team, but the receivers can only advance it. I've seen receiving team players bobble the ball, kick it out of bounds, try to hand it off, fall on it and a host of other results. Every once in a while a player will field the ball and break one off for a long exciting runback. On one such kickoff I do believe that I was looking at a future Bob Hayes as the world's fastest human. This was because this player picked up the ball at about his own three yard line and ran the length of the field, nearly a hundred yards and when I looked up at the clock only about seven seconds had expired. There was 11:53 left on the game clock, or could it be that the operator wasn't paying attention?

It is usually the kickoff and the first few plays when you get a feeling how well the support staff, mainly the clock operator, chain crew and ball boy are going to mesh together with the officiating crew. For example, once the kickoff is over, the chain crew is where they are supposed to be, and the clock operator is on the right page, but the ball boy is fifty yards up field shooting the breeze or looking up in the stands. Now I hate to continually harp about the ball boys but as an umpire I handle the ball on just about every play. Teams, once they see where the ball is spotted on the field, determine where and how they are going to play the next down. The defense will just about always find where the ball is spotted and set their huddle up on that spot and line up their defense there as well. The offensive team will break the huddle and run up to the ball expecting it to be there for them as well. None of this can happen if I have to go chasing all over hell for the ball and ball boy. Unless you have been in the middle of the field with those players you can't see how these types of disruptions can throw off the tempo of the game. As for the best of the ball relays, the other four guys around me take on that responsibility and do so as good as anybody. They know how I work, which basically means that I rarely leave the friendly confines between the hash marks and put the ball down where the wing men tell me to (maybe).

So now you're moving and players are running on and off the field. My responsibility is to count the defense, which is pretty easy to do because I usually set up in the middle of the field until the offense breaks the huddle. This is the time I usually take the opportunity to talk with the kids. I'll ask them how things are going and just make small talk. If I see a kid make a good play I'll tell him so. I want them to know I'm just a regular guy and they can come up to me if there is a problem.

When the offense breaks their huddle, I usually speak to the center right off and see if he has a preference on where he would like the seams of the ball when I put it down. This minimizes any adjustments he has to make prior to the snap. As the game progresses, especially early in the year when it is hot, the ball gets covered with sweat so I always carry a towel to keep it dry. The same can be said for when it rains. Thankfully, it has never happened to me but I read recently where a team came out of the offensive huddle and just prior to the snap the center vomited on the ball and snapped it, at which point the quarterback fumbled it. The only thing that came close was one particularly heated contest where the center was about to snap the ball and an opponent spit on it. We are dealing with kids you know.

By now we are up and running and things are starting to get fun. The players are excited and you kind of feed off their energy. One night a kid came up to me and he was just about sputtering, he was so excited to tell me something. So he pointed to an opposing player and was jumping up and down. I figured the other kid took a swing at him or held him or some other no-no. I sort of gestured to him to just spit it out, kind of like Dean Faber in the movie *Animal House*, when he finally blurted out, "Mr. Referee, that kid made a racial slur!" and with that he turned around and ran off. Nothing more, nothing less.

Like I said, I handle the ball on just about every play and retrieving the ball by the other officials and passing it back to me can be a challenge. Part of the problem is that some of the players watch too much football on television. On a Sunday NFL contest if Jerry Rice misses a chance to catch a ball he turns around and runs back to the huddle. That is the NFL where there are guys standing along the sidelines every five yards it seems with a football to give to the official. Unfortunately, on Friday nights there is one football. But little Johnny watches the game on Sunday and goes out and is playing on Friday and drops a forty yard bomb he figures to do his Jerry Rice and high tail it back to the huddle. One of us has to go shag it and relay it back to where it was snapped from. Every once in a while we tell the player, "Hey, if you ain't gonna catch it, at least go get it."

Of course sometimes the players just get in the way. I can't tell you how many times one of our down field officials has been trying to toss the ball back in to me only to have it hit some unsuspecting player in the helmet. At which point he turns around looking for some wise guy that slapped him in the head.

No Friday night contest would be complete without one of our wing officials tossing the ball right up into the lights, so I am left with nothing to do but duck to avoid a broken nose.

The period between plays allows anywhere from twenty to forty seconds to get the ball ready for the next play. According to the manual there are a whole host of duties that the officials are supposed to attend to in that time. Besides placing the ball ready for the next play, the number on the down box should be changed and the box placed along the sideline where the ball will be snapped next if different than previously. Players on both sides of the ball should be counted and they should be checked to see if their helmets are snapped and mouth pieces are in place. The list goes on. There are a lot of times that things are so chaotic that you're lucky to get the ball placed down and the players counted. Some players see the period between downs as the time to gripe about everything under the sun. It doesn't take an official long to determine if the player is just a crybaby or has a legitimate gripe.

Listening to what a player has to say is part of good preventive officiating. As I may have said before, being an official is not supposed to be about throwing flags but more trying to avoid such things. You have to understand that no matter the level of football that these are just kids and they have a tendency to get a little excited. This is not more evident than at the end of a play. It is eventually going to happen where after a play a player keeps hitting after the whistle. I prefer to step right in and yell loud enough to the offender to stop on the whistle. I try to make face-to-face contact with the player so he can see me and focus on what I have to say. I know officials who will toss a flag or run a kid at the drop of a hat. If after a few warnings or a penalty a player continues to hit after the whistle or any other unsportsmanlike activity, I prefer to let the coach know that his player is on the edge of getting tossed. I figure if this is a player that is essential to this team's success maybe the coach has a little more influence on him than I do. This is especially due to the fact that a few years ago the association adopted a policy if a coach or player is tossed they have to sit out the next game. It doesn't matter if it is the last play of the game. In over twenty years at all levels I can count on one hand how many times I've run a player, and have only tossed one coach.

One year I did the Pop Warner championship game and there was a young kid who was about twelve and he was just a little smartass for his age. He definitely watched way too much football on Sundays because he was continuously getting in opposing players' faces after each play and pushing players who he had already tackled or knocked down. The thing was the kid was a good player and didn't have to imitate some of the hooligans one might view on Sunday. To compound matters this was a close, well-played game even for the twelve-year-olds.

Sometimes my best ideas are those that I get from others and this was no exception. I watched a veteran official pull this stunt once and was so impressed kept it in the deep, dark depository of my mind for just such an occasion. After another incident where the youngster did not stop his aggressive activity after a play's conclusion, I stepped in and signaled a time-out. I was the crew chief at this time and indicated that it was an Official's Time-Out. I did not say another word to the offending youth but motioned him over to his sideline. The befuddled young player followed me as I walked over to where his coach was standing and I motioned to the player and said to the coach, "Coach, this is an injury time-out for this player and he has to sit out at least one play."

Of course now the coach has a bemused expression on his face since the kid looks perfectly all right, so I explain, "You see, Coach, it seems that this player has temporarily lost his hearing since he obviously can't hear the whistle when the play is over. Perhaps you or a member of your sideline staff can restore his hearing before allowing him to return to the game because if he continues to fail to hear the whistle I'll remove him for good." You know, you could have almost seen the light bulb go on as I was trying to do the guy a favor, because the coach kind of winked at me and said he would take care of it. Well, wouldn't you just know it, soon afterward the kid re-entered the game and was not a problem for the rest of the contest. When the game was over, the coach came up to me after the game and thanked me for not tossing one of his star players before he had a chance to set him straight.

Once the game gets going you have to really be alert when you are out there if for no other reason than for your own personal safety. Football is a fast-moving game and today's players are bigger and faster than when I was in school. Being out there amidst all that action, sometimes it can't be helped, but you might get knocked on your behind. One night I was doing a game and about half way into the first quarter the offense ran what looked like a sweep that was headed to my left. It was kind of like a "Student Body Right," where everyone goes in one direction, and all twenty-two players were a good ten yards off to my left.

I don't know where this kid came from but all of a sudden this fullback who was built like a human bowling ball was bearing down on me with nothing between him and the goal line but a forty-something guy with bad knees. By the way he was headed towards me, I had nothing to do but brace for one hell of a collision that would knock me back to Ohio. When he got inches from me, he planted and cut to my right, merely brushing up against me. A few plays later during a time-out, a couple of my fellow crew members were remarking how when that play came at me I had that "deer-in-the-headlights" look, and as I told them how I thought I was a goner they said that they knew that play was coming but could not tell me in time.

You have to be prepared for just about anything. Unfortunately, this might involve an official becoming incapacitated for one reason or another. This is why we try to have an alternate official travel with us. We try to get an official who is about to be moved up to Certified and has a few years' experience. Scott Williams once was our alternate and we had a game at Trevor Browne High School. Not long after the start of the game one of the teams ran a dive play straight up the middle of the field that looked to be stopped for a small gain. All of a sudden the runner broke loose and knocked me right onto my ass. As a result my right knee kind of buckled under me. So I was lying on the ground with my knee hurting like hell and they told Scott to get ready to go in for me. So he peeled off his jacket like Superman coming out of the phone booth and took my place.

I went down right in front of the home bench and I hobbled over to take a seat and there was a doctor right there. It turned out he was an orthopedic surgeon and I seem to recall his son was one of the players or something like that. He checked me out and nothing too serious was wrong. There was nothing broken nor was there any cartilage or ligament damage. The doctor asked me if I wanted him to tape it up and I thought, *What the hell, I'm already here, I might as well try to stick it out.* He did a masterful job of taping my knee up with the exception of the fact that I couldn't bend it. I hobbled back out there kind of like Chester from the old *Gunsmoke* episodes. Scott got a chance to work part of a varsity game and I got a free role of tape.

One thing about being alert during a play also means being in position to be able to see what is happening. For years our line judge has been Harry Sharrock. Harry is not particularly physically imposing. He's kind of short and stocky. When you look at him you get the impression that he might not move too well. Harry knows the rule book by heart and on those occasions when Roger is out of town he has Harry take over as crew chief. I don't know how he does it but no matter what the game situation I can never recall Harry being out of position. I don't care if the play is up near the line of scrimmage or a long pass play forty yards down field; all you have to do is look up and there he is right on top of the play, making the right call. Many times there have been bang-bang plays or a pass interference call that the coaches were adamant Harry got wrong. We'd get the tape and sure as hell he was right there and got it right. It has gotten so we are all kind of spoiled to the point where we just figure if one of us messes up he will be there to sort it all out.

On one night he had me questioning my own eyesight. This occasion the team on offense pulled a sweep to the left and as the runner neared the line of scrimmage I could have sworn I saw Harry right there up on the line, when all of a sudden the running back pulled up and heaved a pass some forty or fifty yards downfield. The ball got batted around and a player looked to have caught it just as it hit the ground. I couldn't be sure since I can't see that far, but there was Harry right there signaling an incomplete pass. I don't know where he came from but there he was. Maybe he can be in two places at one time.

A time was when our crew was scheduled to do a game involving two of the smaller but better high schools. With about two weeks to go in the season our crew was scheduled to work a game between two of the area's Christian high schools. When the schedule first came out we were all kind of excited because this match up was always a good one and as the season progressed both teams were undefeated, and in fact they had met at the conclusion of the previous season and played for the state championship. Both clubs were mostly underclassmen then, so both teams were relatively intact from the previous season. This was during the time that we usually worked four-man crews for varsity games and using a fifth man as back judge was optional. In this case the two schools had agreed to allowing us to use the fifth man. We sure didn't mind having an extra set of eyes out there and the extra official always helps with play coverage.

It was homecoming for the home team and a large crowd was expected as well as some TV coverage, so we were kind of excited as the week progressed. That was until our Commissioner officials dropped a bombshell on us. On Tuesday he called our crew chief to tell him that he was pulling Harry off of our crew to work a game in north Phoenix because one of the officials on that crew had an incident with one of the coaches up there during a previous game. To add insult to injury he replaced Harry with an official who had a reputation for calling every ticky-tack little foul in the book. He was one of those guys who carried something like three or four penalty flags with him and on occasion has used all of them on one play.

We were feeling extremely discouraged that they would pull such a stunt for such a big game. Sure it was two small schools but to those coaches and players it was just as big a game as it was for the larger schools. We met early and had an intense pre-game conference focusing on the sensible use of penalty flags and the advantages of preventive officiating. We took the field and the coach of the home team was a veteran high school football coach and a real gentleman.

He recognized the substitute official right away and you could see the look of exasperation on his face as kickoff approached.

The game got started and on the first four plays this guy had a penalty on three of them, one for clipping during a punt by the kicking team, something I do not ever recall seeing previously nor have I seen since. On the next play on a sweep to his side, two or three linemen ran him over, knocking him out of the contest for good. I mean I have seen officials get drilled and have taken a few good licks myself but this was the toughest I had ever seen. We started out with a five man crew but moved the back judge over to line judge and went the rest of the way with four men. The rest of the game went smoothly and everyone settled down for a good hard-hitting contest that was all we expected. The last I heard, that was the last time that guy ever worked a football game.

A part of being alert and attentive involves knowing when not to blow the whistle. An inadvertent whistle is one of an official's biggest blunders and most embarrassing moments. From the first rules meetings and on through pre-game conferences, that point is hammered home repeatedly; unless you can see the ball in the hands of the runner when he is down, lay off the whistle. There was a rookie official once who said that he had played a lot of football and knew the game inside and out; the last thing he would do is blow an inadvertent whistle. We tried to explain to him that football officiating is not as easy as it looks and to try not act so overconfident until at least he got a few games under his belt. He was not about to be deterred and said that if he blew an inadvertent whistle he would buy us a case of beer.

Not long after that we were doing a freshman game and one of the teams scored just before halftime. On the try for point, just as the ball is about to be kicked Rudy blows the whistle and everybody stops as the ball sails through the uprights. When asked why the whistle, he said he had a penalty, and he said, "The defense did not have enough men on the field." Evidently, the defense only had ten men on the field, at which point we politely informed him that as long as they did not have twelve men or more out there it was perfectly legal and he had just purchased his first case of beer. That first and only season was a rough one for Rudy, who became Rudy Toot Toot because he ended up having to pop for a case of beer about every other game. I think he ended up losing money. It turned out that officiating was not in his future. We were always taking money from Rudy for one indiscretion or another. If it wasn't his inadvertent whistles it was for showing up late. One Saturday morning he was scheduled to work a Pop Warner game with us, but kickoff time came and no Rudy. We ended up doing the game with only two officials. Just before halftime he finally showed up. It turned out that Rudy overslept, which is quite a feat since the rest of us worked a game the night before and managed to make it and he who did not have a Friday night game slept in. At the half they payed us, so we told him we were not going to let him get paid twenty bucks for only doing a half while we ran our asses off. We took half his paycheck on that day. This was how it went for Rudy that first year and it turned out to be his only year. The poor guy ended up losing money for the entire season and got a humbling lesson in the process. You might be the best player in the world when you are in college or high school and you may think you know football, but putting on a striped shirt and going out and officiating a contest is harder than it looks.

Recently, I spoke with my lifelong friend Tom Krispinsky who is a Big Ten official and we were discussing how after years of officiating, you find yourself instinctively watching the officials during a game. He was going to watch a bowl game on TV at a friend's house and I was about to watch the same contest and we agreed that you really do notice the officials and how they keep the game moving. You see them do the little things that the normal fan does not notice, but you do because you know how they fit in the overall scheme of keeping the flow of the game so smooth.

One example of this is at the end of the quarter when the teams switch ends of the field. To most it seems like a little thing but it demonstrates the teamwork of the officiating crew because each member has specific responsibilities at this time. Fans in attendance are paying attention to the band, cheerleaders or are headed to the restroom or concession stand. On TV during this time they cut away to a commercial or some sideline reporter. It is not as simple as picking the ball up and moving to the other side of the field and just dropping it anywhere. If at the end of the first quarter it ends up with the ball on let's say a team's own thirty-seven yard line, between the right hash mark and the goal post with the down and distance third and four yards to go, then when you switch ends of the field that is exactly what it should be at that end.

At the expiration of time at the end of the quarter the referee and umpire meet over the ball and mark the location, down and distance and at that point may verify how many time-outs are left. Meanwhile, the head linesman will meet the chain crew at the sidelines. He will find the spot on the field where the yard line intersects with the chain, at which point he will grab the chain at that spot and instruct the chain crew to basically flip-flop around and go the same yard line at the other end of the field. He will take where he has grabbed the chain and place it on the intersecting yard line on the other side of the field and then have the chain crew stretch the chain back out and they should be at the same position they were before, just headed in the opposite direction and on the other end of the field.

The chain crew member holding the down box should follow the ball and be placed on the appropriate spot on the field. To make sure we get it right, the back judge notes the position of the ball at the end of the quarter and is waiting for us at the appropriate spot at the opposite end of the field. The line judge assists with timing the interval between the periods and observes team conferences and substitutions. He also helps to make sure the ball is placed down at the proper spot. It is usually about this point when we take a good-hearted poke or two at the referee on his "field management ability." Good field management is when at the end of the quarter the ball ends up at the forty-eight or forty-nine yard line, whereby all we have to do to change ends of the field is step across the fifty and put the ball down. Poor field management is when the ball ends up at the two or three yard line and we have to run the whole length of the field to start the next quarter.

In October of 1997 I took a week's vacation back to Ohio and my brother Gib took me to Ledgemont, the high school he taught at, on a Saturday afternoon for a football game. Ledgemont is located about forty miles east of Cleveland in a rural part of Ohio. At the time they did not have lights and played their home games on a Saturday afternoon at noon. First off this was a typical mid-October Saturday complete with cool temperatures and all the fall colors one would associate with northeastern Ohio on an autumn afternoon. Not long after arriving I came to realize that this was the first time in over seventeen years that I was at a high school football game as a spectator, not as an official.

For the first time in a long time I did not have to worry about counting the defensive players or whether or not they were wearing proper equipment and that sort of thing. I found myself enjoying the reds, yellows and oranges of the spectacular fall colors. I took in the odor of popcorn and the smell of hot dogs and burgers cooking and the distant fragrance of someone burning firewood in their fireplace. Since my brother was a staff member of the home team game administration, he got us down on the field as opposed to up in the stands. The kids and parents in the stands were enthusiastic as like any other school and from what I was told neither team was having a great season but to them that game was as important as any other played that weekend.

Before long I found myself focusing on the officiating crew. I know that all officials all across the country have the same Rule Book that I have and get their mechanics from the same Official's Manual I do, but I couldn't help but notice that they do the same things we do. Soon the first period came to an end and as usual most the folks there were focused on the band or headed for the concession stands. I stood there watching the officials as they did their jobs as each are required to do and in a matter of a minute or two the ball had been switched, the chains re-set, the teams turned around and play was resumed without so much as a momentary glitch. From all indications it looked as if the crew was having as good a time as I would have had if I were in their shoes. I went on to enjoy a thoroughly wonderful afternoon and I couldn't help but wonder if they were needling their crew chief about his field management ability.

In officiating we have what we refer as a "good no call!" By this we mean that occasionally there is a play or a set of circumstances that may be easily determined to be one thing when in fact it is something else, but a sharp official recognizes it for what it is and makes the right call as opposed to blowing the play dead when it is not or throwing a flag when in fact there is no foul. One example may be on a forward pass that is barely tipped by a defensive player and afterward the receiver gets hit by a defender, allegedly interfered with had it not been tipped. Having observed the obscure tipping by the defender and not penalizing the interference since once the ball is touched by the defense all pass interference restrictions cease, is a good no call. This often is a gutsy call because in such a case the more severe offense the alleged pass interference is what the players, coaches and fans see not the tipping that negated it. Of course a coach may demand an explanation and having been given one may pacify him; it may not appease a whole grandstand full of spectators who feel they may have gotten the short end of the stick. It always seems that these types of situations never occur when the score is 33-7 but on a play that has pivotal implications during a close contest.

One such call occurred in a game at Sunnyslope High and they were hosting Desert Mountain one night. The game was close and Sunnyslope was trailing by a field goal or less. The home team had worked it to where they had fourth down and goal from the six or seven yard line and were lining up for a field goal try. On a field goal try the line judge goes underneath the cross bar with the back judge to rule if the try is good. As a rule I move to favor the line judge's side of the field in the area he vacates just in case there is a fake or for whatever reason a play comes to that side of the field.

On this particular try for the field goal the center snapped the ball and the holder fielded the ball cleanly. The holder placed the ball down on the tee and the kicker went into his stride and kicked the ball squarely. For whatever the reason the ball never got higher than two feet off the ground and hit the center/snapper squarely in the ass.

Every player on the field stopped as the ball bounced back and forth behind the scrimmage line of the kicking team, but the ball as long as it is still moving around is still alive and at that point there is no reason to blow it dead. I looked up and some big offensive lineman picked up the ball and began to walk toward me to hand me the ball. I can't just tell the player the ball is live because that is not fair, but I am prohibited from taking a live ball from a player, too.

As he continued to walk toward me, I was left with no choice but to back away from him and hope someone else figured it out. Well, now he was leisurely walking from about the eight yard line and nobody else was getting it. He went to the seven, six, five yard lines and I was thinking, *This kid is going to walk in for a touchdown and doesn't even know it.* He got to about the three yard line and I heard the Desert Mountain coach yelling, "Tackle him!" He was still walking toward me holding the ball in front of him trying to hand it to me when finally at about the two yard line two or three opposing players pounce on him and finally the play is over with and he did not score. Although not a lot of the people in attendance that night knew exactly what happened, the five of us knew we had a "good no call." In all the confusion, anyone of us could have blown the whistle and added to the turmoil, but we did not.

One other such incident happened one night and to make matters worse a camera crew from one of the television stations was there. Over the years it truly amazes me how the further a person is from the action on an athletic field, how their eyesight becomes so extremely sharp. It kind of reminds me of the beer commercial where the guy is sitting in the nosebleed section of the outfield upper deck at a baseball game screaming, "He missed the tag, he missed the tag," on a play at home plate. By the same token a fan sitting in the top row of the grandstands can see a play better than those individuals standing right next to it.

We were doing a game at one of the Scottsdale high schools, one of which has a wicked crown to it. It was nearing the end of the game and the score was tied when the visiting team threw a pass that was tipped and just as it was about to hit the ground, it hit the foot of a player who was lying on the ground, bounced up and was picked off by a player on the home team and run back to the visiting team's five or six yard line. When the pass was thrown, I turned to see what happened and just caught a glimpse of it hitting the player's foot, but Harry our line judge was there right on the spot like he always is and saw the whole thing. He laid off the whistle, stayed right with the play and then followed the player intercepting the ball all the way back down the field. Again, a good no call. The home team after three failed tries to punch it in settled for what looked to be the winning field goal with less than a minute to play. With less than ten seconds to play on a last ditch effort, the visiting team had a player run the ball who zig-zagged his way sixty-seven yards down the field for the winning touchdown with no time remaining. While it looked like the interception was to have led to the winning score, it turned out that it didn't have an effect on the outcome, but regardless we all felt pretty good that either way we got it right.

That lasted until shortly after the game when we all went to a local restaurant for burgers and beer and the ten o'clock news came on. On the Friday night sports they have highlights of the local high school games and right up there on the television were the highlights of our game. When it came time to show the crucial interception play, the camera was at ground level, across the field and set up in the end zone. The play was up at about mid-field some sixty yards away. With the distance and the high crown of the field, the player on the ground was barely visible, let alone his leg that the ball bounced off of. With the camera angle being what it was, it looked clearly like the ball hit the ground and bounced up before the home team player intercepted it. Of course the sportscaster couldn't miss the opportunity to poke fun at us because the tape allegedly showed us missing the call. We all knew that the Commissioner liked to watch those newscasts and would probably have seen what we just did so it would come as no surprise if Roger got a call Saturday morning wanting an explanation, but we worried about that as long as it took for the next pitcher of beer to arrive.

It's not that we take a dismissive attitude toward such things. It's just that we have come to the realization that we are human and we know that in this instance we got it right, but there are times when we may miss a call or two. The key is to understand that these things do happen and when they do just admit it was a mistake and move on.

Think about it. The players don't make perfect blocks on every play. Coaches don't call the right play 100% of the time. Personally, this is why I don't particularly care for instant replay. If a team has fourth down and inches and the coach calls a quarterback sneak and it comes up short, he can't say, "Well, let's just do it over and I'll punt this time because the sneak was a bad call!" If a kicker has a chance to win the game with a last-second field goal and the holder bobbles the snap and he shanks it to the left, he can't ask to re-snap the ball and try it again. We are all human and not perfect and that should be part of the game. I did a game once and on a play to the sideline I saw a defensive player give a kid a shot a good five yards out of bounds. So blatant was the hit not only did I flag it but the line judge tossed his flag as well. After marking off the fifteen yards and with only seconds left in the first half, the team with the ball attempted a field goal that cleared the cress bar by only inches.

The next day the game was tape-delayed on television and when they showed the late hit out of bounds the defensive player definitely made a move to hit the player out of bounds but missed touching him by inches. Had we not marked off the fifteen yard penalty the last second field goal try would never have cleared the bar. I felt bad that the team got three points it did not earn, but both of us were where we were supposed to be and saw what looked to be a foul. It was a mistake is all. Not my first and definitely not my last.

As officials we may not take ourselves too seriously but one area we do is player safety. Some years ago there was an extremely unfortunate incident where one of the local youths died suddenly at high school football practice. One of the precautions that were emphasized afterward was to keep the players hydrated with lots of water. It has gotten to the point that if need be the game officials are authorized to call an Official's Time-Out at any point in the game if we feel the kids need water. When the season starts in Arizona it is usually 100-plus degrees at kickoff and doesn't drop too much as the game progresses. This lasts until sometimes mid-October.

As an umpire in the middle of the field I pay close attention to the players and if they look a little woozy I stop the game in a heartbeat. I'll talk to them and ask them how they are and even some times a teammate will tell me if someone isn't doing so well. The coach is taken completely out of the equation when it comes to player safety. Gone are the days when water is withheld from the players to toughen them up. But there were a few old school coaches left that tried to hold onto that line of thinking.

One such coach was at a game one night and it was a brutal night. It was hot and unusually humid for Arizona, and just before halftime there was a called time-out by the visiting team whose coach was one of those old school dinosaurs and he came out to talk to his team. We instructed both sides to bring out water for the teams. Now time-outs are supposed to be only a minute but in this circumstance we allow as much time as necessary to bring out water for everyone. To be honest I often use this as a chance to take a few slugs on the old water bottle and may even douse myself on occasion to cool down. On this particular night the water-boys were a little slow getting to old hard ass's team and as he was leaving the huddle, he ordered them off the field, saying, "My players don't need water!" It is just this type of thing that the policy was adopted for and not only did the water-boys not leave the field, they stayed out there until everyone got their fill of water, including me, and then were they allowed to return to their sideline. That coach has since retired and hopefully the likes of him as well.

I knew that if I was going to write about high school football, the subject of coaches would fit in extensively. They are as big a part of the game as any other component. Like players, coaches will try to emulate the coaches whose personality they marvel at.

There was Jerry Glanville, the former pro coach who was shown on ESPN berating an official on the sideline, saying something to the effect of, "Do you know what the NFL stands for? Not For Long if you keep making calls like that one!" It wasn't long afterward that some Pop Warner coach was using the same line in a Pee Wee youth game although I don't know where the NFL part applied at that level.

But like them or hate them coaches are a big part of the game and you can't go around making enemies of each and everyone of them. There may be certain coaches that no matter what you do you can never satisfy them, but there are people in all walks of life like that. Most of us have found that if the coach has confidence in your ability the less likely they are to challenge your decisions.

Early in my career I learned there was no quicker way for a coach to lose confidence in your ability as an official then to be unsure in your calls and your conduct. One of my earliest instructors told us of a method by which to demonstrate confidence by what he described as "selling the call!" This official who had also been a baseball umpire gave the example of an umpire behind the plate making a call giving a really weak hand signal and offering up a meek strike call. He then demonstrated the same by which he offered a strong, confident hand signal and a firm, decisive, "STEEERRRIKKKE!"

He then cited an example in football that if you have a penalty take and throw your penalty flag with authority and confidence, don't just take it out and drop it like, as he put it, "like some hooker down on Van Buren Street." Anyway, the message was to be sure of your calls because if you are wishy-washy and uncertain it will give the coaches the impression that you are not confident.

One example of "selling the call" came one afternoon in a freshman game at Alhambra, and on the last play of the first half the home team was trying a short field goal. This was one of the rare games where I was working as a line judge and was under the goal post to make the field goal call. The ball was snapped and the kick was blocked. I only know that because as soon as the ball was kicked I heard it hit something or someone. I was a good forty yards away and the next thing I heard was a whistle and the half was over. When we got together at the half we had a discussion and from what I understood the referee had a momentary brain fart. When the ball was kicked it was rolling around on the field. Just about that time a member of the opposing team was about to pick up the ball with nothing but green grass and white lines between him and the goal line. The referee somehow got the situation confused with a try for point after a touchdown where once an opponent gains possession of a botched try the play is blown dead. Before anybody knew it both teams had left the field and the referee did not call the teams out for an Untimed Down, which should have been the case. The amazing thing was that absolutely no one said a word or even noticed what happened.

The rest of the game continued and luckily it had no effect on the outcome. The only one who said anything was as I was walking to my car after the game and a man in his fifties with a set of binoculars came up to me with a girl in tow who had to be half his age and asked me why that play was stopped after the botched field goal try, and I kept removing my whistle and other equipment like nothing had happened. Without missing a beat I very matter-of-factly stated, "A blocked field goal try on the last play of the first half, the ball is automatically dead." Of course this explanation was total bullshit and completely improvised at the time.

I must have been pretty convincing because as I was putting my gear in the trunk of my car the same guy walked by arm-in-arm with his lady friend and I heard him saying, "You see, honey, if there's a blocked field goal try on the last play of the half, the ball is dead."

There are a lot of officials that do more than one sport and for a while I flirted with the idea of becoming a basketball official, but my reluctance I think goes back to when I was in school. After getting my ass kicked for three months of football practice in junior high, the prospect of another several months of basketball practice after school just did not appeal to me. Even though I was growing like a stink weed and enjoyed basketball, I just wanted to relax at that point. The same thought process came into effect with respect to becoming a basketball official. There was a whole set of rules meetings and clinics to attend not to mention a test to take and although I probably would have enjoyed the games, all the other stuff associated with it seemed a bit too much at the time.

It didn't keep me from sharing stories with those who were sports officials in other sports than football. One thing that is apparent is that no matter what the sport or what level you are at, there are going to be coaches where no matter what you do they just don't get it. I think that probably goes for all across the country as well. This matter is not helped when aspiring coaches see highlights of college or pro coaches throwing chairs across a court or tearing up sideline markers and tossing them onto the field. Just before a JV contest one night a coach came up to us and said he had a question for us.

What he said was a question was actually was an opportunity to bitch about football officiating in general. This guy was about seventy-five years old and said he was a "football purist," whatever the hell that was, but in his opinion officials in general did a lousy job in that they did not call all penalties during a contest. In his eyes he thought that every foul no matter how trivial it might be should be called. We tried to explain to him that especially at the frosh and JV levels the skill degree is not as refined as it is at the varsity level and that the purpose of football at this level is for the players to gain practical experience. It is the goal of a good official to spot minor infractions and talk to the players in an effort to teach them the proper way for the games to be played. The message we tried to communicate to him was that penalties, unless the foul leads to a distinct advantage to a team, should be used only if discussions with players fail. To take a point of emphasis from my earliest of mentors, "You enforce not the letter of the rules but the spirit of the rules."

No amount of good reasoning would dissuade the coach as he really felt in his heart that no matter how insignificant the foul he expected it to be called and if the game took four hours to play well, so be it. If we had to mark off a penalty after each play that was fine as well. Once the game got started he let us know it. To add to the turmoil for being a "football purist," we began to wonder what sort of football he was a purist for. For a guy that wanted every rule enforced to the letter, he sure did not know what rules they were. If a player shifted positions, no matter how legal, he wanted an illegal shift called. Every forward pass was made beyond the line. Every block was a hold or a clip.

Sometimes when dealing with an individual of this nature, an unconventional approach might just work. If anything the predictable methods have failed, so why not try? I read once of a basketball official who had a coach that was riding him relentlessly. Now let me just say I have a lot of respect for basketball officials. Football is tough enough with the fans being separated by the sideline and the running track. In basketball they are right up on top of the official. Anyway this basketball official had a coach on his ass, and after a foul call the coach jumped up screaming his head off and throws his clipboard up toward the ceiling of the gymnasium. His having already nailed the coach for a previous technical foul, a second would result in his being ejected. So the official looked over at the coach and said, "Coach, I'm not going to call a technical on you... that is until that clipboard hits the floor!" I guess the sight of the coach racing frantically around the floor trying to catch the clipboard before it hit the ground was pretty hilarious even though he was unsuccessful. Either way the official got the coach off his case.

As to the "football purist," just as the half ended he came storming up to us presumably to bitch about the officiating, but before he could get out a word Roger stopped him and said, "Coach, I've got one question for you, what color is the rule book?"

The "football purist" was speechless. It seems that the National Federation publishes a new High School Football Rule Book each season and the cover is a different color each year. Only if you are completely familiar with the rules and keep up after them each year (as we as officials do) will you know the color from year to year. The "football purist" wandered off mumbling to himself and we didn't hear as much from him the second half.

CHAPTER VIII

HALFTIME!

You have gotten the first half of football under your belt and it is time for intermission. Once the final seconds tick off, the umpire takes the ball and holds it over his head, signaling the end of the period. Before leaving the field, the clock operator sets the scoreboard clock for fifteen minutes. Once both teams have left the field, the referee signals the clock operator to wind the clock and the halftime interval officially begins.

Once the officials make their way from the field they have to locate the guy with the key, again! You only have about fifteen minutes to take a break and the more time you wait for the guy with the key the less time you have to relax. In the most ideal of circumstances the guy with the key is waiting for you as you leave the field and escorts you to the dressing room. Even better yet, when he lets you in, there is an ice bucket awaiting you in the room with a half dozen or so cold sodas in it. Believe you me, after a whole half of chasing those players up and down the field, especially early in the year when it is so hot, the sight of an ice bucket with cold drinks floating in it is pure delight. All I can think of is those old, grainy, black and white cowboy movies I watched as a youth where the cowboy has lost his horse and is crawling through the desert sand and spots the oasis up ahead, but it only turns out to be merely a mirage. At least the ice bucket and contents are for real.

I don't know what the reason, but no matter how hungry I am I can't eat anything at halftime. I think it goes back to my high school days. On the first day of double sessions when I was a sophomore I had one too many bowls of cereal and after the initial laps that began practice and calisthenics I found myself off in the corner of the practice field with an upset stomach. Luckily, I survived and used the experience to educate myself as to my eating habits prior to strenuous exercise.

Some guys give in to their cravings and that is all well and good, but some folks' eating habits down right bewilder me sometimes. One day I was working a Pop Warner game with a guy and it was late in the day. This was at a site where there are three of four games going on simultaneously. But by this time all the fields had cleared off and our game was the only one in progress. The concession stand was totally out of food and this fellow was ravenous. As usual I just had a soda and was happy with that, but as I looked around my hungry counterpart had disappeared. I looked around and he was nowhere in sight, so I began to slowly make my way back to the field. I caught a glimpse of him exiting the convenience store across the street from the facility carrying a paper sack. Upon his return he reached into the sack and took out a package of hot dogs among other various food items. As he began to unwrap the package of frankfurters I told him we didn't have time for him to cook up a couple of hot dogs, at which point he indicated he had no intention of heating them and proceeded to begin eating them one by one, completely raw. Ever minding his manners, he graciously offered a few to me, which I politely rejected. He broke open a bag of pork rinds, wolfed them down and washed the whole thing down with a can of orange soda.

At the half when the door is closed and we are given some privacy, after a minute or two we sit and re-hash the events of the first half. Were there any plays that occurred where maybe we could have covered it better? At this point if there are any adjustments to be made then we make them. On one such occasion the entire chain crew walked in and said they had to go. No reason at all they just up and quit. So we have to scramble to find a new crew.

On more than one occasion I have spearheaded an effort to fire the ball boy. On one occasion in Superior, a copper mining town about thirty-five miles east of town we had a young boy of about ten who was one of the coach's sons. He was way too young and way too inattentive to be given such a responsibility. The first half dragged on because we incessantly had to search out the ball boy on each change of possession and on some of those he gave us the wrong ball. We agreed the ball boy had to go and the start of the second half we had him replaced. He spent the rest of the half sitting at the base of one of the light poles, moping the entire time.

There used to be a high school in east Phoenix at 44th Street and Thomas called Gerard Catholic. One game there we had to replace the clock operator and keep the time on the field, but not for the usual reasons. The clock operator had been located at a card table in the corner of one of the end zones. Most clock operators are up in the press box at mid-field. To make matters worse this game was late in the season and the football field had been reduced to dust. Whoever coined the phrase "three yards and a cloud of dust" would have been in his splendor this night. Every play in the middle of the field, and there were a lot of them, resulted in a huge choking swirl of dust and dried grass clippings. So thick was the haze along with his station on the field, the poor clock operator could not see through it to see us signaling time-outs or the referee winding to start the clock. Once the game was over I discarded the socks I wore rather than even attempt to wash out the thick layer of dirt that had encrusted them. Anyway we saw that the current set-up was not working and to make matters worse we were dying out there choking in the dust. The clock operator was really understanding when we told him we had to try another method of timing and we kept the time on the field.

I can't remember how it came about but the responsibility of keeping the time was delegated to yours truly. The entire second half was like playing in a dust storm with officials and players alike coughing and choking after each play. It got to the point where nobody was having any fun and it seemed the only way that there was going to be any reprieve from the conditions was to just get the game over with. Of course the coaches, who were standing on the sidelines not exposed to the same degree of brutality as those in the middle of the field, didn't share in that thought. Well, what they don't know won't hurt them, so on those occasions where the clock was supposed to stop I would take my good old time in reaching down to my wrist where my watch doubled as a timer and stop the clock. When it came to starting the clock I would do so without hesitation, maybe even a little early.

You would be amazed how rapidly the game moves along when you shave off a few seconds here and there. You throw into the mix a little good old teamwork such as telling the linesman and line judge that on plays along the sideline where it is borderline if the play is in or out of bounds that perhaps it would be best if the ruling was inbounds to keep the clock moving. This I should emphasize is not to be done recklessly and is only meant for extreme circumstances such as these. Although this method of moving the game along has been implemented a few times over the years, my colleagues have recognized me as the pioneer of what will from that day forward referred to as "timing dynamics."

Halftime is intended as a break for the players and it is great that the schools use this opportunity to showcase the bands and dance lines. It is usually about half way through the season that the schools have their homecoming. Just about every school that hosts homecoming extends halftime by at least a good five minutes. This is usually to include some type of ceremony during the intermission. When I was in school it was to crown the homecoming queen. These days I have seen halftime celebrations that involve floats and fireworks displays and are much more elaborate than those when I was younger. Over the years I've known some officials who see this as a big pain in the ass. As a person who was not a big athlete or very popular in school, I can recognize the value of these ceremonies, especially in light of the fact that a lot of the schools try to include as many members of the student body in the festivities as possible as opposed to limiting the celebration to just a select few.

As a game official, the only cause for concern is that because of the extended period of inactivity, to make sure that the players have an ample opportunity to warm up once they return to the field. The rules call for a three-minute interval for the players to warm up. This period is in addition to the fifteen minutes that run off right after the half is over. Each coach is supposed to have his team out on the field before this three minute time frame, but invariably one or both coaches will be so absorbed in his halftime speech that they lose track of time and rarely make it out in time. Although the rules call for a penalty to be called on the offending coach, it is rarely called. We usually wait until the teams are both on the field and then start the three minutes. Maybe the coaches might think their players don't need the warm up and stretch; I let them have that opportunity.

When I was in high school the Youngstown Board of Education fell on financially hard times so the public high schools cut back on extra curricular activities in an attempt to save money. As a result most of the schools did not have marching bands so much of the halftime activities for the football games had little or no halftime entertainment. In fact had it not been for out football coaches doing their jobs for free there would have been no football season.

It has been some thirty-five years later and every once in a while there will be a game where there is no big halftime show. Well the temptation of a vacant, lighted football field along with all those footballs lying around the sidelines it doesn't take long before you have a few kids come out from the stands and start throwing the footballs around. One night it might have seemed like a good idea for one kid but that soon changed in a heartbeat.

During a game at Washington High there was a lull in the action and two or three kids began to throw a football around. Another kid came out to join in the fun and lo and behold it was none other than the little fat black kid from the Pop Warner Saturdays at Central. If you will recall he would show up every Saturday and raid the concession stands but stopped showing up suddenly. Well here it was a year or two later and he was indeed alive and well. By now he was about twelve and had to be about 5'4" and close to 200 pounds. He was standing at about mid-field yelling for one of the other boys to throw him the ball. One boy standing about thirty yards away let it fly and heaved a toss skyward. I mean he really threw it high and long, almost like an infield fly ball in baseball. So the little fat kid stood at mid field for the ball to come to him and at the last moment another taller and leaner young chap ran in front of him, he too trying to catch the same ball.

He leaped high in an attempt to grab it but was a split second too late and just managed to tip the ball. He did, however, manage to change the trajectory just a bit and instead of a nice tight spiral the ball began to tumble end over end. Having the flight of the ball changed ever so slightly did not result in the portly youth making a spectacular catch but instead it hit him right in the balls. Everyone who was looking at the sight let out a collective gasp because as the guy in the beer commercial says, "That has to hurt!"

Immediately the other kids came running up to him and asked if he was okay and he gingerly made his way to the sideline and the only response he managed was a very meek, high-pitched, "I'm all right." The last we saw of him, he was walking past the tennis courts that were behind the field when an errant tennis ball came bounding harmlessly in his direction and he avoided that thing like it was a World War II hand grenade.

Getting the kids off the field at halftime is just one of the tasks officials have to do before the second half can get started. If they haven't done so already, you have to get the band off the field. Now that doesn't sound like all that big a deal and it isn't usually. That is unless you happen to have a band director that takes offense with the fact that his perfectly good band concert has to be interrupted by a stinking football game. At one far north valley high school one night we had a band director who did just that. He had a program in mind and he was not going to give up until it was completed. We finally had to enlist the aide of the athletic director before we could get the game under way. That would have been weird enough in its own right, but what would follow later that night would just put an exclamation point on an otherwise mediocre contest. More on that later.

Once the teams are out and the three-minute warm-up period is completed you have to go round up the captains again for the second half choices. The captains are brought out to the middle of the field and they shake hands, at which point the referee will point out that we have had a good half of football and it is up to captains to set an example for the rest of their players. The team that lost the opening coin toss or deferred is given their choice, that is if they know what their choice is. Occasionally a captain will forget what he wanted to do so you have to give him a little help. As with the start of the game, we talk to the coaches and will ask them what they want to do with the ball if it's their choice. Before we used to do this, we had a captain come out for the start of a second half and his team had lost the opening coin toss. It was now his choice to start the second half and he chose to defend a goal with the wind at his back. We asked him twice if he was sure that was what he wanted and he said he wanted the wind at his back to start the half. When he got to his sideline his coach was beside himself. It was true he wanted his captain to choose to defend a goal but he wanted the wind at his back in the fourth quarter. It was a close game and he figured it might come down to a last minute field goal.

Sometimes the half is delayed for reasons that are a little less traditional. One night we did a game at North High, an inner city school in central Phoenix. Before the game, the school administration informed us that there had been some gang problems at the school during the week and there had been a threat of a drive-by shooting sometime during the game. As a result they decided to beef up security at the school that night. "Beef up" was an understatement; there were more police and school protective service personnel there that night than there were folks in attendance. Just before we brought out the captains for the start of the second half there was a loud "BOOM!" that came from the northeast corner of the stadium. Everybody froze for a moment. As it turns out it was no drive by shooting at all but what has to be the stupidest drunken driver in history. It seems that some drunk was going down 12th Street and tried to make a left turn and plowed into a utility pole. To make matters worse the guy tried to flee the scene of the accident on foot. The only problem was that there were more cops in plain clothes and unmarked vehicles outside the stadium than there were inside. He was quickly scooped up by authorities and everyone gave a sigh of relief and the game resumed without incident.

I hate so say it but there have been incidents where concern for one's personal safety has cropped up and they are not all at inner city schools. Not all have taken place at varsity games on Friday nights. Lately I have read in a few nationwide publications where there are well-placed concerns over the deterioration of sportsmanship in youth sports.

I have always said that when being a football official ceases to be fun then that is time when I will get out. It is for that reason that I do not do Pop Warner football on Saturday mornings any longer. Don't get me wrong, the kids are terrific, but the parents and coaches are another matter. I used to officiate flag football which is meant for the six- and seven-year-old variety. Believe me it is an accomplishment to get the kids lined up for a play, let alone introduce anything too complex. These kids are just learning the game and it wasn't unusual for a little tyke to come up to me and ask, "Are we winning?" In one game we had to keep escorting one little guy to his proper side of the ball because he was mesmerized by the airplanes taking off from the airport nearby. But the parents are another story. If you call a foul on little Johnny, they like to kill you.

At a game between Phoenix Christian and Bourgade Catholic, after the game some drunk came up to us screaming you, "Goddamn fish-eaters," implying that we slighted our calls in favor of the Catholic school. This ass was the father of one of the players and here was the poor kid pleading with him to settle down and he was just getting worse. A police officer working the game came over to escort us off the field and he started in on the officer. We made it to our dressing room and when we emerged afterward the guy was gone. I don't know if they carted him off to jail or what but he deserved it. I felt sorry for the player since not only did his team lose the game bit he was embarrassed by his drunken horse's ass of a dad. The most surprising thing about that whole incident was that both of those schools have faultless reputations for sportsmanship.

Like I said earlier we as a crew don't like to throw a lot of penalties and it is just before the start of the second half that Roger reminds us that the first one to throw a flag in the second half has to buy the beer afterwards. It is usually about now that he begins to take suggestions on where we are going to go for our post-game eats.

CHAPTER IX

ARE WE DONE YET?

Your second half of football is under way and just as we as officials have made adjustments, sometimes the teams have done so as well. Some coaches for one reason or another have made adjustments to their kicking game in particular punt returns. I only mention it because I see this happen so frequently I can just imagine how it makes the coaching staff want to pull their hair out. What I am referring to is the decision not to return back a punt and to just let it roll down until it is whistled dead. Sometimes it is because of weather conditions (yes it does rain in Arizona) or maybe his special teams have not been able to field a punt cleanly or hang onto it. In any event I have seen the coach send out his punt receiving team with the explicit instructions to his players to stay away from the ball once it goes down field. It never ceases to amaze me no matter how forceful the coach is in his instructions to his players, there is always one kid who just doesn't get it. I can be in the middle of the field and hear the coach yelling at his players to stay away from the ball once it is kicked. It has gotten to the point where I can almost pick out the one kid who is going to mess things up. He is usually some player who gets in a few plays a game, his uniform is not dirty and he is usually the one who just before the whistle blows plows into some unsuspecting opponent who is standing ten to fifteen yards from the play and then stands over him like some sort of big hitter.

So the ball is snapped and the punter will get his kick off and down field the ball will go sailing and the receiving team will figure out where the ball is headed and just about everyone will stay away from it. Of course out of nowhere here comes one member of the receiving team hanging around the area where the kick is coming down. Now this is where the individual who designed the shape of the modern football has the last laugh on the rest of the world. Unlike other action sports like basketball, soccer or baseball that use a nice round ball that has at least some degree of predictability as to where it will bounce once it hits the earth, footballs are more oval-shaped and have pointed ends that make it spring up in countless unexpected directions. I cannot prove it but I swear the ball has a directional device that causes it to deliberately seek out unsuspecting receivers in just such a set circumstances.

Invariably the kick will hit the ground and along comes the one and only player who has not obeyed his coach's order to stay the hell away from the ball. It is at this point, like the ball had radar, that it will bounce up hitting him in the leg or back, at which point the kicking team will pounce on it and gain possession at that spot. When this happens if you look quickly enough to the sideline you can actually see the lines etch into the coach's face or his hair turn grey. The recovering team will be holding up the ball and celebrating while the one player who caused the whole disarray will slowly return to his bench with the typical "what-just-happened?" look on his face. This just doesn't just occur in the high school games; I have seen this at every level.

In November of 2000 I was on vacation back in Ohio and had occasion to attend the Youngstown State University and Southern Illinois football game in Youngstown. In the second half YSU was in the process of squandering a 21-0 lead when SIU punted and when it came down it hit a YSU player right in the head and the Salukis recovered deep in YSU territory. From there they went on to rally and win the game. That was Coach Jim Tressel's last home game at YSU and from there he went on to win the National Championship at Ohio State. I on the other hand had just traveled over 2,000 miles only to cry in my beer.

Probably the most bizarre of these punting foul ups came on Halloween night a few years back at a game at South Mountain High. They were hosting Carl Hayden and both schools were having a rough year and each school stood a chance to win the game which was played during a heavy rainstorm. The ground in Arizona for some reason is not designed to absorb large amounts of water. They say it has something to do with it having once been the ocean floor way back when. In any event the field at South was soaked and every time a kick or punt hit the ground it just sort of flopped there like a high pitching wedge hitting a really soft green. The score was tied and it was late in the game and the Carl Hayden defense had held and stood a chance to get the ball in some decent field position. The Carl Hayden coach was pleading with his players that if they did not block the punt to keep away from it once it got down field.

The teams lined up and South snapped the ball and their punter got off a good kick that looked like it was going to land at the Carl Hayden forty yard line or there about. I look down field and there were about four or five white-shirted South players in the area and sure as hell there was one kid in blue and gold standing about five yards from where the ball was about to come down. Every other kick that night just sort of hit and stuck right there but this time I swear this kick had to hit the lone dry spot on the entire football field and instead of hitting and dropping like a dead duck, bounced and skipped sort of like the rocks Andy and Opie threw along the lake at the beginning of *The Andy Griffith Show*. The ball hit the kid from Carl Hayden right in the face mask and before he could realize what happened a South player swooped down and recovered it at about the thirty-six yard line. Of course they went on to score and win the game. After the game the coach from Carl Hayden was surprisingly composed and even said how he thought his team really had a chance there. I figured he was referring to winning the game and it turns out he meant to score an offensive touchdown. I guess you take your success wherever you can get them.

There are times when a player should go get the ball and they don't and of course that too can be frustrating for all involved. Every once in a while a team will come out and in an attempt to catch the defense off guard will throw a pass out in the flat to a wide receiver out near the sideline. Since most of the players are all bunched up in the middle of the field the idea is that with only a few defenders out in this area the chance to break a play for a long gain is always a possibility. The problem with these types of plays is that as soon as the ball is snapped the quarterback just steps up and throws the ball to the sideline. If he is not careful, in his attempt to get the ball to the sideline the direction of the pass is often parallel to the line of scrimmage or even backward. If that is the case and the receiver does not catch the ball and it stays in the field of play it is still a live ball and can be picked up by virtually any player and advanced. In this situation it is imperative that the official on that sideline lay off of the whistle, as mentioned before a "good no call." In the case where the pass is parallel to the line of scrimmage, the receiver gets confused thinking it was a forward pass and just does nothing. He thinks the play is over. It is not unusual to see a defender jump on the ball or pick it up and in that case it is his team's ball.

The worst example of this sort of blunder I have ever seen came in a game that I was watching, not officiating. I did remark at the time how the officials who were working that game kept their cool and called it properly. It was in the late '70s and I was at a game in Niles, Ohio, on the sidelines taking pictures. Niles was playing nearby Howland on the last game of that season. The QB from Niles received the snap from center and threw a pass out in the flat to a receiver who was just off the line of scrimmage. The pass was just barely backward but definitely backward nonetheless. The receiver dropped the ball and I to this day couldn't believe what happened next.

The Niles player who did not catch the ball began banging himself in the head, obviously frustrated over not catching the pass. The ball was rolling on the field a few yards away and I thought to myself, *You know, I didn't hear a whistle and that sure looked like a backward pass, why doesn't someone pick up the ball?* Well, this kid from Howland must have read my mind because he came out of nowhere and scooped up the ball as it rolled around, and ran the length of the field unscathed for a touchdown. This whole play unfolded right in front of the visiting Howland team's bench, so understandably the whole sideline erupted when their player crossed the goal line and the official signaled "touchdown." The Niles player who committed the original slip-up was looking around bewildered at what all the excitement was about, but only when he returned to his sideline did the gravity of his lapse finally sink in. The poor kid was crushed and it only got worse; the game wore on and the Howland touchdown resulted in the game's only score and they won 8-0.

Having come out on the short end of a lot of football games I often think sometimes it is worse to lose by a close score than to get your ass kicked on a lopsided contest.

In a game that is a blow-out, the frustration factor for the team on the short end of the score has a tendency to escalate rapidly with the score. Most of the classier coaches who are up by a bunch will usually keep it on the ground and start substituting reserves for starters before too long.

What really bothers me is when a team is up by a huge score and a coach will keep his starters in there and run up the score.

My old high school was not a football powerhouse as I have said, so I know what that feels like. To this day I tell people that I am from Ohio but not a big football fan of Ohio State University football. Part of it goes back to the fact that when I was growing up, it was not like today where college football games receive the exposure that they do on TV. Unless you wanted to see a college football game in person, there was the local Youngstown State University games at old Rayen Stadium. To watch OSU you had to hope the game was on TV or drive three hours to Columbus, so I became a big Penguin fan and remain so to this day. But I think subconsciously I had a little ax to grind with the home state Buckeyes when one year they played Michigan and were whipping the hell out of them and late in the game Ohio State scored again, and to rub salt in their wounds went for the two point conversion. After the game someone was interviewing Buckeye Coach Woody Hayes and asked him why he went for two points when he had such a commanding lead. His response was, "Because I couldn't go for three!"

In one contest the losing coach came up to us between the third and fourth quarter and asked to reduce the time from twelve minutes to ten to shorten the game. The opposing coach was against this saying he had players who had not played much and he wanted to get them into the game. But, when play resumed he had the same players in there that he started the game with. He continued to utilize his starters and kept running up the score.

The state association has adopted a procedure at the three lower levels to eliminate this sort of occurrence. Now if a team is ahead by forty-two or more points after the halftime the game is stopped at that point.

Even at the Pop Warner level if a team is down by twenty-five or more points, after a score there is no kickoff. The team that is down gets the ball automatically at the fifty yard line.

At the two highest levels of football in the state there is no such procedure and coaches are free to run up the score if they so desire. In these cases an official has to really keep after the players and maintain order. I often find appealing to the player's sense of personal pride helps. Rather than allowing a player to get caught up the emotional part of the defeat, I try to emphasize that he is a good player and is better than that. On the other hand my fellow crew members and I are quick to tell the players to get back to their huddle once the play is over. During one such game the winning team was frequently taunting the losing team who were exercising incredible restraint, and finally near the end of the contest a couple opposing players were mocking the losing team when Roger just blurted out, "Don't listen to them, they are a no class outfit!"

In very few cases a blow-out can be satisfying. Every once in a while a team needs to be taken out behind the wood shed and given a good old fashioned ass-kicking.

There was one northwest valley high school that for a few years had a decent football program but for some reason changed coaches. A year or two later their program went down hill and they were a .500 team at best. Their new coach was a heavy-set, dark-haired guy who looked a little like Jackie Gleason and was always bitching about something. Wait, I stand corrected, one of his assistants was always bitching about something.

Let me point this out, if there are any coaches out there reading this it is time to let you in on a little secret. We sports officials are a lot smarter than you give us credit for. We know for example that each of you has a designated screamer. This is the assistant or assistants whom you appoint to do all the yelling at us that you are too unwilling to do yourself. Thus, if you run up against an official or crew who isn't willing to put up with their shit it will be the assistant who will get tossed and not yourself. We also know that you head coaches can count which is substantiated by the fact that every once in a while you or one of your underlings will come storming onto the field during a time-out and announce something to the effect of, "You know that's nine penalties against my team and only one for them!"

When we toss a flag against your team we don't get together and say, "Well let's throw one against the other team to keep it fair." Sometimes we run up against teams that just aren't too disciplined; your team might just be one of those teams.

Well Jackie Gleason's team played a team from Glendale that was way undermanned and he pummeled them something like 62-7 early in the year. Even in the rout his sideline kept complaining about everything. You know it is a little like the kid who cries, "Wolf!" When the real thing comes along nobody is there to listen. The same holds true to the designated screamer. Somewhere along the line there may just be a legitimate issue brought up and it gets lost in all the other bullshit. So there they are running up the score on a team that they could have easily have let up on to the point where they are trying fake punts in the fourth quarter. His players were a bunch of smartasses but not to the point where they were doing anything illegal. Oh I guess one could interpret some of the heckling as "an act that engenders ill will." But if we started doing that it would have just extended the contest longer and the best thing to do in that case was just to get it over with and move on.

Way later in the last week of the season we got this team again, this time they were the home team. They were hosting one of the Yuma area high schools and that year all the Yuma schools were having great seasons and the valley school was headed for a sub .500 season. At the half the Yuma school was up by a bunch and we had decided that if the game kept up in this fashion that late in the game we would let our alternates work the last part of the fourth quarter to get some of the field experience, especially with having an unreasonable coach on the sideline. But before that we had decided that our stout friend on the home sideline got a bit of his own medicine for a change. We vowed that as long as we as a crew were doing the game we weren't going to make any effort to shorten the contest. At the start of the second half there was a delay because the band would not leave the field as mentioned earlier, but under the circumstances we didn't mind because the home team was in for a long half as the tables were now turned. They, like the Glendale team weeks earlier were the team undermanned and were going to get a good old fashioned ass-kicking.

About half way through the fourth quarter the home team was down about 35-3 and we were just about to allow our alternates to rotate in the game and give each of us a few plays off. Of course the home team's assistants were bitching about everything possible but it was a pass play in the end zone that was the most memorable. On what was the home team's deepest penetration into the opponent's territory they had fourth down and about five yards to go on their opponent's twenty yard line. The quarterback dropped back and let loose a pass in the end zone for what looked like a sure touchdown. A defender came across the field and arrived just as the ball and receiver were about to meet. He popped in front of the receiver and got his hand up just in time to poke the ball away at the last moment. Having his only real scoring chance ruined, the home coach was infuriated and it just had to be our fault.

He came storming out onto the field, positive that there had to have been pass interference and we were singling his team out for some undisclosed transgression. Opting not to use one of his assistants as his puppet on this occasion, he was hopping mad and bellowed, "That is the worst call in the history of football." Imagine that! Ever since the day the guy picked up that soccer ball and ran with it, ours was the worst. I swear the guy looked like Ralph Cramden when he threatens his wife ,"To the moon, Alice!" I guess that was supposed to enrage us but all we could do was laugh at this idiot. By this time a good portion of the few people who were in attendance took off so there was not a lot of crowd noise. We couldn't help but chirp among ourselves how we had made gridiron history and how we hoped that would put us in the record book because it was after all "the worst call in the history of football." It seemed that the coach had a case of "rabbit ears" and heard our barbs, which was just good-nature needling amongst us, not aimed at the coach. He didn't see it that way and continued to fume the rest of the game, but our train of thought was *to hell with him*. I don't remember, when I signed on to be an official, forfeiting my right to free speech. Besides, this guy was getting a well-deserved ass-kicking and I was having too much fun.

It wasn't long and the game was over and we showered and left. Harry owned a bar not far from the school and we went there for food and beverages and as we sat at a table I realized that I had mistakenly taken one of the school's towels with me and had it draped around my neck. In the spirit of the moment we figured the National Federation probably would not recognize our achievement of having made the worst call in the history of football so we took matters into our own hands. We took the school's towel and got out a magic marker. In big letters we inscribed the date and time along with the final score with the phrase "Worst Call in the History of Football." We each autographed it and Harry hung it on the wall of his bar with the other sports memorabilia and I think it still hangs there to this day.

As for the coach he got fired soon after that and the next year he was an assistant at a different school.

We continuously tell the coaches to control their sideline and they try to keep everyone back and it is more a safety issue than anything else. Late in the game, especially a close one, they tend to lose focus and bodies creep perilously close to the sidelines. One of our fellow officials got seriously hurt once when he was covering a play that was headed out of bounds and got tangled with someone on the sideline and ended up tripping over the pole vault track that ran parallel to the football field. He fell and severely broke his wrist. So you can see why we harp on the coaches to clean up their sideline. Players usually keep within their team box but the cheerleaders, statisticians and others have a tendency to roam up and down the field.

Dealing with coaches can get to be exasperating especially when there is pre-game baiting going on. At every level of football you hear of remarks made by one team or another that is used as "bulletin board material" that more often than not results in more enthusiastic play by the target of said quips than anticipated. Coaches, too, have a tendency to do that. There was one coach at a Tempe high school who had a tendency to shoot off his mouth and there was a local sports network that featured high school football games and did a pre-season interview with this coach. He was bragging as usual about his team and Arizona high school football and made the remark his team and Arizona teams were as good as any in the nation. Like my dad used to emphasize to me, a little humility goes a long way, but then this guy never met my dad and I thought he was a loudmouth. Nonetheless, somehow they ended up scheduling a game with his team and a team from central Pennsylvania, a mediocre team from central Pennsylvania no less. Well, his team that he claimed could compete with anybody got their lunch handed to them. As an official you may end up hearing about such nonsense prior to a game and it's just something else you have to watch out for.

There used to be an older black gentleman who was an official with our association, Big Willie Jarvis. Big Willie stood about 6'5" and went about 250. He was a big quiet man who had an infectious smile and he substituted for us a couple of times. By the time we met up with Big Willie he had lost some of his speed and he had a tendency to be out of position from time to time. One night in a game at South there was a play down the field right by the end zone and near one of the sidelines and the play headed his way, but Big Willie wasn't moving out of the way. You just wanted to yell to him to get the hell out of the way but there was not enough time. So the play ran right over him and the next thing we saw was Big Willie knocked flat on his ass with his arms extended what would have been skyward had he been upright signaling touchdown.

On another occasion he worked with us one Saturday during a Pop Warner game. At the Pop Warner level the games are played anywhere they can fit in a football field and goal posts so sideline control is a huge problem. In some places all that separates the sideline from the field is a flimsy yellow rope. On this particular afternoon it was late in the game and I was on the opposite side of the field from where Willie was and the team on offense was moving from my left to right. They were on about the twenty yard line of the other team and they ran a sweep to the other side of the field. Again, the play headed right for Big Willie who was standing right on the sideline. Now from where I was standing it looked like all he had to do was take a step or two either to the left or the right and he would have been in good shape, but he didn't.

Now these weren't real big kids but even a whole pile of twelve-year-olds slamming into you can knock you for a loop. Just shy of the sideline the runner was surrounded by about a half dozen opponents and the whole pile just kept moving in Willie's direction where I could see he was absolutely going to get knocked head over heels. Not far beyond the direction in which the whole pile was headed I caught a glimpse of something shiny and metallic, but before I could make out what it was Willie and the object disappeared from view after a loud clank. As I have earlier said, after turning forty my eyesight isn't what it once was and I was sure this was the case again as I could have sworn I saw a man-sized figure tumbling through the air.

Literally, once the dust settled further investigation revealed that as Big Willie was being driven out of bounds he was knocked into about a ten foot high folding step ladder that had been set up not far from the field. Every step ladder I've seen lately comes with a printed warning to never stand or sit on the top step. Well obviously some folks don't heed warnings too well because perched helplessly atop of the ladder was some guy with a video camera who was taping the game. The aluminum folding ladder was no match for Big Willie who steam-rolled over the ladder with ease, sending the unsuspecting parent tumbling to the ground and separating him from his video camera. Miraculously, no one was hurt in the collision other than a couple of bumps and bruises. You can just about rest assured that further attempts to capture any sporting events for posterity will be done from a safe distance in the future, at least for this one gentleman. I would have loved to have seen that tape, though.

Anyone who has been a football official for any length of time will admit that there are times when you just get fooled or as I say "fall asleep at the wheel" and can get caught out of position. You are human and subject to making mistakes. But, be it for laziness or whatever the reason to continuously do that makes the other officials have to work harder and looks bad. To try to make up for the mistake by covering it up is even worse.

There was an official who was notorious for letting a play get by him and then would compensate for it by calling the play back with a penalty. The official, who always had huge bags under his eyes, looked like he needed about thirty-six hours of sleep. I saw tapes of a few of his games and there would be a long play down field and there he would be up near the line of scrimmage a good twenty yards out of position. On the tape you would see what looked like a yellow bird flying through the air and it was what we would refer to as a "Sleepy's Rainbow" since it would be him tossing a penalty flag some twenty-five yards for some minor indiscretion that would call the play back. It would be for some petty offense but he used it to make for his lack of hustle.

We have always felt that it just makes us feel awful if late in the game an official's call has to affect the outcome of a game. This is why we try to be proactive and talk to the players and try to head off just that sort of thing, but sometimes you have to make a call that has an effect on the outcome of a game and often it is an unpopular call. That is when you have to suck it up and do the right thing.

One such incident that took place was a game in the mining town of Winkleman, one of those towns where the whole city turns out for the high school football games. They were playing a team from Florence who had about a thirty-game winning streak.

This was a close, hard-fought contest all night long with no team clearly pulling ahead and late in the fourth quarter the Winkleman home team scored and took a narrow lead by less than a field goal. After the ensuing kickoff Florence had the ball inside their ten yard line. They had a pretty good kicker so all they had to do was get in field goal range and stood a good chance to extend their winning streak.

On this one play their quarterback took the snap, dropped back to throw and was standing about five yards deep in his own end zone. He threw a pass that was caught at about the forty-five yard line and the player then ran into the opponent's territory. But back in the end zone where the ball was thrown from, just as he released the ball one of the opposing players who was rushing the passer changed direction to head up the field. One of the passer's teammates took off charging right at the opponent who now had his back turned to him. Roger was screaming at the kid not to hit him but in the heat of the contest the Florence player wasn't listening. He got a running start and just leveled the opposing player, nailing him from behind. The opposing player was standing two to three yards deep in the end zone and the deeply flagrant clipping foul was obvious. Flags flew and once the play was over we brought the long pass play back. If that wasn't bad enough the foul was by an offensive player in his own end zone. The ramification of that is any foul by the offense where the enforcement spot is his own end zone the result is a safety. So not only did the foul negate a fifty yard completion, Winkleman was awarded two points, the ball was placed on the twenty yard line and Florence had to kick the ball away to the opposing team. After doing so all the home team had to do was run out the clock and the winning streak was over.

After the game we saw the Florence coach headed in our direction and I figured he was going to really let us have it given how the game ended up. He was naturally upset but more so at his player than at us. The foul in the end zone was so obvious that he saw it from as far away as mid-field where he was standing. He said to us that he was hoping that we didn't see the illegal block but it was so obvious there really was no way we could have missed it. Considering the circumstances he was quite composed. Now if he stayed that way once he got his team behind closed doors is another thing.

One game we did at a Tempe high school had all the signs of being a rout with the visiting team leading 23-6 at the start of the fourth quarter. This was one of those games where we as officials look at one another and scratch out heads and say, "I guess that's why we're not coaches." The home team came out to start the game and ran the ball all over the place and jumped out to a six point lead. They continued to run the ball until they got near the goal line and then they started throwing the ball all over the place. At that point they let the game get away from them and the opposing team scored twenty-three unanswered points. They stayed with the passing game until the fourth quarter when they went back to grinding it out on the ground. It was a little too much too late and they scored sixteen points and closed the gap to 23-22, but with only two seconds left in the game.

Our whole crew was preparing for what we knew would be an onside kick, so we were all on our toes for what might transpire. The teams lined up and once the referee gave the signal that it was okay to kick, the kicker kicked a low line-drive kick that hit one of the up linemen of the receiving team. As soon as the ball touched a member of the receiving team the clock started. After striking the opposing player the ball bounced up in the air a good ten to fifteen feet. The ball seemed to float up there for what felt like an eternity. When it finally came back down a member of the receiving team gained possession and tried to run with it.

In high school football a member of the kicking team may recover a free kick if it goes ten yards or is touched by a member of the receiving team, but he may not advance it. As in this case the play was blown dead and as it turned out the game clock had expired. The home team tried to contend that there was one second left but the ball was in the air a good two seconds aside from the time the players scrambled for it once it came down. Mark, our back judge who was watching the clock verified that and we raised the ball signaling the game was over. Given the manner the home team had staged its comeback, that did not sit well with some of the home team faithful. Nonetheless, the game was over and we headed for our dressing room. That was one of the Tempe high schools that got it right in that they have a Tempe police officer escort the officials on and off the field and true to form there were two Tempe officers waiting for us at the edge of the field who led us to our locker room.

Once we were safely in our dressing room we showered, dressed and were packing up to leave. I couldn't help but notice that the police were still in the dressing room and it was a good half hour after the end of the game. I asked why he was lingering back with us since I was sure he had better things to do than hang with us and he said he was going to wait and escort us to our cars. I figured that maybe there were some hostile fans and he wanted to assure our safe departure and he said that was not the case. He said that once we were out of the dressing room he and his partner were going to come back and arrest the football coach. It turns out that this was the last game of the season and a pretty unsuccessful one at that. I guess the manner in which the game ended just added to a whole season of disappointments. The frustrated football coach went into the coaching staff office and trashed the place and they intended to file charges against him for destruction of property but wanted to wait until everyone cleared out before doing so.

Heaven knows what causes coaches to make boneheaded decisions, especially late in the game. My brother Gib is a life long New York Giants fan and to this day still laments about the "Miracle in the Meadowlands." Anyone who is a pro football fan has seen the countless replays of this play where the Giants late in a game against the Eagles had a narrow lead and with little time remaining all they had to do was have the quarterback take a knee and the game would have been won. Instead, a running play was called and Giants quarterback Joe Pisarcik in an attempt to hand the ball off fumbled. Eagle defensive end Herman Edwards scooped up the fumble and scored the winning touchdown. I was watching that game back then and sat in disbelief as the play unfolded before me on the TV.

I don't know what they were thinking then and don't know what they were thinking of years later at a game at Arizona Lutheran who was leading a game late and they too had to merely have the quarterback take a knee to assure themselves of victory.

On this night apparently whoever called plays for them was not aware that football is played east of the Mississippi and had never heard of this infamous play-calling bungle. But on this night a new level of ineptitude was surpassed when I saw what unfolded before my eyes and those of my colleagues. With only seconds remaining the ball was snapped and the quarterback, of all things, dropped back to pass. He tossed a pass off to his right in the flat which was picked off by a defender. The momentum of the throw nearly carried the player out of bounds but he regained his balance only to return the ball back up the sidelines inches from the white-lined edge of the field. He continued to tightrope his way untouched up the field some fifty or more yards to score the winning touchdown with no time remaining. While the visiting team celebrated their last-minute victory the home sideline was devastated. A few of them argued that the defender stepped out of bounds but the truth of the matter was that had the quarterback just taken a knee the game would have ended differently and whoever called that play was the real goat here. We walked off the field shaking our heads once again saying, "That's why we are not coaches."

To me the term "crunch time" has a special interpretation. For me that is when you are in the midst of a close contest and it is getting late in the fourth quarter. Like I may have mentioned that we officials every once in a while fall asleep at the wheel and miss a call or blow an inadvertent whistle. It happens to the best of us. But at crunch time you take that whistle out of your mouth and pay extra close attention to what is happening around you. Keep your hands in front of you and if you begin to reach for that back pocket where you should keep the flag by God you better throw it. I saw a guy one time late in a game who was running down the field and began to reach for his flag but just as he was about to do so had second thoughts and didn't throw it. Unfortunate for him he was right in front of the team box on his side of the field and man did they ever give it to him.

It was a rare Saturday night game when Seton Catholic played Scottsdale Christian at Seton's home field in Chandler. Again we had a substitute official with us and this fellow was the head linesman who was touting the fact that he was a junior college head linesman and this mere high school contest was purely child's play for him. This was back when we still used four officials for a high school game so the linesman and line judge were responsible for calls down field.

The two schools involved were small at that time and there were only about a hundred fans in attendance so needless to say it was a small crowd there that night. As Roger likes to say, "It looks like another late-arriving crowd." But, even though it was a pair of small schools and a small crowd, the game is still important to the twenty-two kids out there playing it. So late in the game when the score was tied the plays at the end of this game mean a hell of a lot to these players just as much as in the big games.

Our substitute official who I have never worked with before or since was of the mind set that since I was an umpire I did not have the mobility that a junior college linesman possesses. That may be the case, in fact I probably don't have the mobility of most JV or varsity linesmen, either. It seems that over the years I have learned that umpires do not necessarily have to be world class sprinters but maybe having a little bulk comes in mighty handy when you are in the middle of a bunch of guards, tacklers and defenders intent on knocking each other all over the field, so if he has blinding speed well, good for him. I don't mind a little needling from the guys on my crew but when a total stranger whom I don't know is the culprit, he is not ingratiating himself to me. Remember what I said earlier about a little humility when working with a new crew, well this is the reason behind that standpoint.

This brings us to what I refer to as "crunch time" where the game is on the line and if there is a time to pay attention to details this is the time. The game was tied and it was the fourth quarter with only a few seconds to go and coming up was what should be the last play of the game. Seton had the ball up at about mid-field so we were gearing up for what was probably going to be a long pass play. The ball was snapped and the Seton quarterback rolled to his right in an attempt to pass, but there was a fierce rush and he couldn't set himself to throw the ball. He eluded a tackler and stepped up towards the line of scrimmage. An umpire on a pass play has to step up to the line to assure that the passer is behind the line when he throws the ball. This passer was getting dangerously close to the line but just before crossing it he stopped and let loose with a long pass. As I was looking down the line of scrimmage I managed to spot something out of place, the head linesman. Normally, on a pass play he should be down field to rule on catches and pass interference fouls. But, for some reason there he was.

The quarterback had just heaved a long pass down field as far as he could throw but as the ball reached the high point of its arc there was the shrill tweet of what was unmistakably an official's whistle. Just about all the players stop and down comes the ball right into the arms of a Seton player standing in the end zone for what should have been the winning touchdown. So not only was the linesman out of position, he ran into the middle of the field and announced that for some unknown reason he had an inadvertent whistle. To make matters worse he was right in front of the Scottsdale Christian bench when he did so and their coach at the time was an individual who was not known for his self-control to begin with. He heard the whistle blow as did every oneelse and his main concern was to get that winning touchdown off the scoreboard. Since there was no band to blame it on, the referee had no choice but to give the signal for an inadvertent whistle which is basically holding your fist out extended with the thumb up.

An inadvertent whistle with no time remaining is treated the same as a penalty in that the game cannot end on that note, thus requiring an untimed down. We had to interrupt the home team's celebration and bring both teams back out onto the field for one more play. The scoreboard operator had to take the six points off the board. In the ensuing down Seton tried another Hail Mary pass but the Scottsdale team was ready this time and it fell well short. This was before we held a playoff to settle tie games so the game ended in a tie. The home Seton team was obviously downtrodden since what looked like the game would have ended with a win now resulted in a tie. Afterward in the dressing room the official responsible for the inadvertent whistle could only offer "I blew it" as an explanation for his slip-up. Like I said, a little humility goes a long way especially when you think about going out there and amplify your ability, and then go and make a horseshit call.

CHAPTER X

THE GAME IS OVER

The final gun has sounded and hopefully you haven't fallen victim to stray gunfire. Once again you probably have to go seek out the guy with the key. Before you can get back to your dressing room to shower and change you have to make your way back there in one piece. There are occasions where that is an adventure.

It is on those occasions that a sports official learns you cannot please everybody. In over twenty years I have been fortunate that I have never been the subject of a physical assault but I have heard of occasions when such an incident has taken place. In recent years there have been some heavily publicized incidents where sports officials have been attacked by parents or fans and it is disturbing that it seems their occurrences are becoming more and more frequent.

Recently, I recall a couple of drunken fans who attacked an umpire at a baseball game had received national attention and before that I seem to have read that a father attacked an official after a youth hockey game. It has even gone so far as one afternoon I was watching a TV talk show in which the host was a psychologist. He had a mom on his show whose daughter was in a youth softball league and the daughter wanted to quit the team because she was drained as a result of her mom's constant intrusions into her softball experience, especially badgering the shit out of her coach in a dispute over the coach's management of the team. This mother had gone as far as pulling her daughter off a team that she didn't think was best suited to the needs of her daughter and having her join a different team. Just as the poor daughter got used to a new team and new friends along came Mommy Dearest who got pissed off at the coach for one reason or another. I presume the coaches if they have any stones at all would tell her to kiss their asses. You could tell by the look of anguish on the daughter's face as they kept cutting away to her as her mom and the host covered her constant interference. I guess it is the habit of this particular show to extensively utilize video cameras to follow the subjects of that particular day's show and document some of the behavior leading up to the telecast.

They showed video tape of one of the daughter's ball games and this woman would take up a position right behind the backstop clearly within earshot of the home plate umpire. Throughout the contest she continuously berated the umpire, the opposing players and her own daughter at her lack of success. I marveled at the self-control of the umpire because I wanted to reach through the TV set and strangle this loudmouthed blowhard of a mother. The most astounding part of this whole broadcast was that the mother thought nothing of her behavior even though her daughter was over-wrought with frustration as was her husband who refused to go to the games as a direct result of his wife's behavior.

I have to admit there are times I get pretty sick and tired of some of the abuse directed at officials. One night I did a JV game and one of my fellow officials was a rookie. Earlier I mentioned that the schools get a sheet in the mail with the officials' names and level. A "four" means a newer official and one of the assistants must have figured it out and he was on this kid's case all night long. Now this coach from Westwood was one of those Napoleonic individuals suffering from Short Man's Complex. Their team lost this game and he heaped the entire blame on the new kid and kept it up even after the game was over. The new official didn't quite know what to make of this guy since I guess this was the first time he had some ass riding him relentlessly. As we were leaving the field we all got together since we officials have a habit of leaving the field together just as a precaution.

As the fence surrounding the stadium approached, this little jerk continued his tirade at the new kid so I simply asked, "Do you intend to keep this shit up all night?" He said something to the effect that we all weren't good enough to work varsity games on Friday night so we were relegated to only messing up JV and frosh games. I merely pointed to the opening in the fence that led to the parking lot and said, "He being new thinks he has to listen to your bullshit. You might be tough shit out here but once I hit that fence this striped shirt comes off where you are just another loudmouth asshole and all bets are off then!" Before long a couple of other coaches grabbed ol' Napoleon and ushered him away from us and we made our way to our cars without further ado.

It never ceases to amaze me what people will come up with to complain about. At North one night a drunk up in the stands took exception at the manner in which Roger was running the clock. We were never quite sure if the game was too fast or too slow for his liking but he made a point of coming down as close as he could get as we left the field at the half to lodge his complaint. He kept screaming at Roger, "You can't run that clock for shit!" He was still there as we returned, yelling the same thing. Between the third and fourth quarter somehow he made his way down to the field and there he was as we switched ends of the field, still yelling, "You can't run that clock for shit!"

North High had a struggling football program for years and this was no exception. They were getting trounced and we had already decided that we were going to keep the clock moving so as I was putting the ball down at the new spot to start the fourth quarter, I said to Roger, "Boy, that guy thinks your clock mechanics are really shitty."

At this point he yelled to the guy, "Just watch this quarter if you want to see shitty."

People who attend athletic contests have a right to their opinions, but one Saturday after a Pop Warner contest this guy who looked like the movie character Ernest came up to us and told us what a terrible job we as a crew did and how we screwed up the whole game for his kid's team. Soon afterward another guy came up to us from the opposing sideline. This guy was a black man who looked kind of like Richard Prior and he proceeded to tell us we sucked. The first guy told him he didn't know shit and that our rotten officiating spoiled the game for his kid's team, not the black guy. The black guy said he knew football and he knew we sucked and that Ernest had no right to bitch and if he had a problem with that they could settle it out in the parking lot.

It looked like both these men had a little too much to drink and that in itself was an accomplishment since it was only about eleven o'clock in the morning. So Ernest proceeded to stand his ground that our sucky officiating had more of an effect on his kid's team and he had no problem taking the matter outside and vowed to kick his ass. Now Richard Pryor told Ernest, "You better kick my ass because if you leave me standing I'm gonna go into the trunk of my car and get my gun and kill your ass!"

At that point we went up to the concession stand where they keep the phone. They don't have security at Pop Warner games so we told the gal running the concession she might want to call the police because there were two guys out in the lot about to fight over who thought we sucked more and one of them was threatening to use a firearm to emphasize his point.

The lady working the concession stand looked at us with this "yeah-sure" look on her face. I then said, "Look, lady, out there in the lot are two guys ready to go at it and one of them said he has a gun, maybe he doesn't, but if he does do you want to accept the responsibility for a young kid getting shot in the crossfire?" Evidently, she figured I was not pulling her leg and went for the phone. A while later I went out to my car and there were three or four Phoenix police cars in the lot and they were talking to the two men. Hopefully, one or both of them were headed for jail.

On a few occasions there will be a person that will come up to you and pay you the ultimate compliment. That is after a good, hard hitting, close game between two quality teams that there will be a coach, spectator or school administrator who will come up to you and say, "You know, guys, we hardly even noticed the officials out there tonight." That is how we hoped every game would turn out, where we are invisible and nobody even knew we were there.

Once you have returned to the dressing room there is the guy with the key and he usually will ask you if you need anything else and I never thought it was a big deal but you might have to ask for hot water. One year we were scheduled to do three varsity games at Tempe High. It is an older school a mile or two from Arizona State University. The first game there was early in the season when it is a hundred degrees at kickoff. Once the game was over we went to take our showers and there was no hot water. Anyone who has spent any time in the Arizona heat can tell you if you turn on the cold water in your faucet it doesn't come out cold very often as was the case on this night, so it wasn't that bad. In fact early in the season when it's so hot a little cool water is refreshing after running around in the heat for two hours.

The second contest was later in the season in October and the temperature cooled down by about twenty degrees. The game was over and we went to take our showers and again no hot water. This time the water was cold and all you could do was kind of dance around under the showerhead a bit and rinse yourself off. This was not refreshing at all.

The third time we went back there was in November and the outside temperature was about fifty degrees. I don't know if your blood thins out living in Arizona or what but coming from northeast Ohio I never thought that I would find fifty degrees on November a cold day but it is. When I arrived to do the game I asked the guy with the key specifically about the hot water. I told him that the previous two visits there was no hot water and tonight especially I had hoped there would be hot water for our post game shower. He let us into the dressing room and he returned after a little bit with some towels and he guaranteed that there would be hot water. Once the sun went down the temperature dropped another ten to fifteen degrees and was really chilly. When the game was over I was looking forward to a nice hot shower. We got to the dressing room and I jumped into the shower and jumped right back out because the water was ice cold and I froze my ass off.

The opposite of the cold water situation is the one where your game is at an older school and the plumbing system is really old. Because of this we have a rule. When one or more of us are in the shower *do not* flush the toiler. This came as a result of a night at one of the older copper mining towns. After doing our game we were showering and someone was in the toilet and when he flushed the toilet the cold water was evidently diverted there momentarily and we were just about scalded by the sudden surge of steaming hot water.

With the game over we often sit down for a few minutes and go over any plays that were out of the ordinary and how we could have improved our coverage. There will be a play where the question of how we applied a rule may come into the discussion and you would be surprised how many times we have to look it up in the Rule Book to see if we called it correctly. Usually if there is an Observer present he will come in and give us a summary of their report. Most of the time we will listen to their critique because after all they are officials, too. As I have mentioned there are a couple of these guys, the Casper Crew, if you will, that I took exception to.

One night we did a game at a northwest valley high school. The opposing head coach at the time is an old friend of Roger's and had just had a major surgery. Did this stop this courageous coach; not one bit! Somehow they rigged up this kind of contraption that was a cross between a wheelchair and an elevated bed. He had to be wheeled on and off the field and he would sit up at about mid-field where he could watch the game and call plays from there.

The visiting team won a close game and as we were leaving the field Roger who had not seen his friend since he had the surgery wanted to go over to him to say hello and ask how he was doing. I went over with him and we stopped to see him briefly. I had never met the man and Roger introduced us so I could take a moment to applaud his courage.

After the game we got to the locker room and there was the NFL ass-kisser member of the Casper Crew. This night there was no former NFL alumnus working with our crew for him to toady to, so he lit into Roger right from the start. Without waiting for an explanation he jumped right into him for what looked to him was Roger going over and congratulating the winning visiting coach. Almost in stereo we both responded to this accusation that this was not the case but a genuine expression of concern for his ailing friend. I had little admiration for this obese sycophant and had even less from that point forward.

In fact in the years to come I would have more than one football official tell me that they were opting to discontinue their officiating career specifically because the opinions of these Casper Crew members were held in such high regard by the Commissioner that they felt that advancement through the officiating levels of promotion were being compromised. Some of these officials demonstrated a high degree of competence and I felt that their loss was going to be detrimental to the overall level of officiating as a whole. I heard horror stories of officials being promoted not because of their on-the-field ability but rather how they looked in their uniforms.

I know a guy named Albert who coached baseball and when he wasn't, devoted his full time duties to his law practice in Phoenix. His practice was so big at the time he had an office in Yuma. He knew a fellow attorney down there who was also a football official. One day I was telling Albert that I was working a paid chain crew for one of the smaller State Championship games being played in the Phoenix area that Friday night. He told me that his buddy who we'll call "Rick" and his crew was assigned a State Championship game up here, also. Albert had heard me berate the Casper Crew on more than one occasion and the word of their exploits had reached the Yuma crew assigned to the game. On the night of the game it turns out it was Rick and his crew working the game at a Tempe high school. Just before taking the field, in walked my least favorite Observer complete with his huge beer gut, bulbous red nose and typical golf shirt with the NFL logo on it.

Now let me say this right off the bat. I knew that officials everywhere that are assigned a State Tournament final in any sport are pretty much be the cream of the crop. A mediocre or bad crew stands little chance to work a contest of this magnitude. On our way out to the field I spoke with Rick and told him what my thoughts were, but not to hope for a glowing evaluation from the individual who was observing them.

I thought this crew did a good job in the game except for one or two slip-ups that didn't have any effect on the outcome of the game. Once the game was over the Observer came into the locker room. Now keep in mind that the drive from Yuma to Phoenix is three to four hours so these guys had a long day and it wasn't over yet. But this Observer took a full hour ripping these guys and I just sat in a corner taking it all in as I had been in this situation a time or two myself. When he finally was done we showered and were walking out when Rick said to me, "You know, I find it hard to believe that in two and a half hours we didn't get one thing right!"

My response was, "Now you see what we're up against."

After the game was over and we had showered, we were ready for the most important part of the night, where were we going to go eat? Over the years we developed a few favorites and just about wherever we go in the metropolitan Phoenix area there would be a favorite eatery or two that we would go to after the game. Nothing against restaurant chains, mind you, but it just seems that the little neighborhood joints have a certain flair to them. For example, Roger teaches at Madison Middle School located on North 16th Street and frequently we will meet him at the school and pile into his Jeep Cherokee and take off from there. You could just about bet your life if you wanted to find any of us on a Friday when Madison School was the jumping off point for us, if you went strolling in the Wineburger on 16th and Camelback you would find us there.

The Wineburger is just a little hole in the wall that is an older place set next to a car wash which is long closed by the time we get there so parking is never a problem. It is just a bar with about fifteen to twenty tables and booths that serve mostly a neighborhood crowd much like the ones that were on South Avenue in Youngstown where I grew up. Maybe that is why I like to go in there so much or maybe it is because they have really good burgers there, I don't know their secret and to be truthful I don't think I want to know. When I was a kid just out of high school I did what any other kid did in Youngstown, Ohio, and that was go to work in the steel mill. That was before I became a cop, and just around the corner from the Youngstown Sheet and Tube there was a joint like the Wineburger that served the best burgers. One night the owner's son who was also the cook had finished his shift in the kitchen and was sitting at the bar tossing back a few drinks, so I asked him, "John, what is the secret about how you get that special taste to your burgers?"

He replied, jokingly I hope, "I never clean the grill." From that day forward I figured that some things are just not worth knowing.

That is the way it is all over town. If we do a game in north central Phoenix we go to a place called Tommy's for pizza and wings. But Friday night at Tommy's is also karaoke night which means that we get the rare treat of listening to Hank Morris sing. Now I can't carry a tune at all and I would not think of getting up in front of a crowd and sing and the first time Hank did it I thought he was going to make a fool of himself. I thought I would fall over, I mean the guy really can sing.

On nights where we have a game in Paradise Valley or Scottsdale we stop at Brennan's Irish Pub on Bell Road just down from the Paradise Valley High School. Each table has a vertical wooden peg attached to it where the waitress puts a roll of paper towels. This is required for the wings they serve there which come soaked in sauce, the heat factor to be determined by the patron. Believe you me that roll of towels begins to unravel frequently once your order arrives and we usually order up several batches ranging from mildly hot to burn-your-ears hot. By the time we are ready to leave all that remains on our table are empty pitchers, piles of wing bones and crumpled paper towels.

On those rare occasions we get a game in the east valley over in my neck of the woods, none other than yours truly does the cooking.

Now some may find it hard to believe but I like to cook. When the crew come out my way I usually throw a corned beef brisket in the crock pot and by the time the game is over and the guys get to my place it is done and among other things I fix them hot corned beef sandwiches. Afterwards we go out on my patio and enjoy a post game cigar, another one of our vices, although Mark the back judge just chews on his.

You may think, *This guy isn't much of a cook if all he does is throw a corned beef brisket in a crock pot*, but I really do know how to cook some things, just ask the crew what happens every New Year's Day, more on that later.

Car rides home themselves can lead to adventures. We were scheduled to do a game in Payson, a city about sixty miles northeast of the valley up in the mountains. This was back when we made the old timer Elmer give up his driving duties and we had Harry drive that day. He borrowed a car from I think his brother-in-law. On the way home we were coming down the hill from the mountains when the oil light on the dash came on. Before long the engine died and we managed to come to a stop in front of an old gas station that looked abandoned on the Fort McDowell Indian Reservation. Of course there was no phone at the darkened station. The station sat not too far from the road that came from the Indian Gaming Center that is now a casino but back then was a Bingo Parlor that the East Valley elderly used to flock to. It was not long before the place closed and a line of cars came down that road, so it looked like we might find some help. And it was help we would need because Roger, Harry and I had Pop Warner football games the next morning at 8:00 a.m.

There must have been at least fifty cars come down that road loaded with blue-haired little ladies and not one of them would lift a finger to help us. Pretty soon the flow of cars coming down the dirt road slowed to a trickle until it was obvious there were no more to come. After a while another car came down the road and from the silhouette our spirits were lifted as we saw the familiar outline of a police car. It was Tribal Police car and they stopped and we explained our dilemma. In the car were two Native American cops who said they didn't have a telephone in their car which was no surprise since this was back in about 1984 before cellular phones, but they sure as hell had a radio, but it was clear they had no intention of using it to assist us.

A few miles up the road was the town of Fountain Hills that had a few twenty-four-hour businesses that at least had phones and we asked could they give one of us a lift up there. Of course this was a foolish request since it was too much effort to get them to press the button on a police radio, imagine the inconvenience of having to have to expend some effort to actually help someone, but they did say they would check on us from time to time. With that they drove off. By now it was after midnight and we were sitting there figuring out what to do next. According to the sign on the window, the station was scheduled to re-open at 7:00 the next morning if in fact the station was still in operation. A worst case scenario was that we stuck it out until morning and called for help when the place opened and the Pop Warner game would have to go on without us.

At about 12:30 in the morning a pickup truck pulling a camper pulled off the road into the gas station to adjust a tarp covering the truck bed that was loaded with camping gear. The guy that got out of the driver's side looked just like Charles Manson and he was traveling with this light skinned black girl who was covered with all kinds of tattoos of the Devil and other assorted snakes and demonic likenesses. Harry asked the guy if he could give him a lift to Fountain Hills but that was in a southerly direction and he was headed to another town up in the hills, Heber, which was up north and he wasn't willing to turn his rig around.

This guy had all kinds of stuff in the bed of his pickup so we asked him if he had a quart of oil in there. He said he could sell us a can of oil and he said he could part with one quart of oil for five bucks. A real bargain considering a quart of oil back then was going for about sixty cents. So now we had a quart of oil that hopefully would get us going but alas, no way to open it. Seeing our dilemma the good samaritan suddenly sported a big grin and said, "Let me help you with that." He then reached behind his back and pulled out one of the biggest knives I have ever seen and stabbed several holes in the top of the can. The manner in which the guy wielded that knife had me convinced that this fellow could easily carve us to bits. We thanked him for his help and to our relief he was on his way. We put the oil in the car and it didn't make a difference. The car would not turn over. At this point we we're all just standing around when someone noticed that there were three or four concrete monuments by the side of the road. I couldn't help but remark, "That is probably the last officiating crew that got stranded out here."

Roger and I found an old school bus behind the garage and managed to get the folding door open and decided to try to get some sleep. At about four in the morning we were awakened by the sound of a vehicle pulling in on the gravel beside the bus. While we were sleeping Harry managed to hitch a ride to Fountain Hills and called his brother-in-law who drove out in his pickup to get us. Roger and I climbed into the bed of the pickup that was covered by a camper shell and a spare tire was just lying in there with hay strewn about. I thought if it was good enough for the infant Jesus some 2,000 years ago it was good enough for us. Roger and I used opposite sides of the tire as a pillow to sleep in during the last leg of the trip back into town while Elmer and Harry rode up front.

I finally got back home at about 5:30 a.m. and ended up making it to the Pop Warner game with about ninety minutes sleep in my own bed.

Back before we retired Elmer there was a period of time where we got a few games on the far northwest valley. As a rule we always tried to ride together but for some reason Elmer would set out on his own. I didn't give it much thought until one night we did a game at a high school not far from Sun City. Elmer finally told us that he found this night spot off of Grand Avenue in Sun City that catered to the folks in the huge retirement community. It seems that he would go down there and mingle with the unattached ladies that frequented the joint from what I am told is quite a large contingent. A single, active old gent in these types of places pretty much has his pick with the ladies and Elmer who was a widower evidently found this out and was going to take advantage of it to the fullest. Unfortunately, Sun City is not a cheap place to live or to socialize but it seems that he had a solution for that, too. He was not about to imbibe in an establishment that sold cocktails at such inflated prices but having had a few drinks under one's belt loosens you up especially when on a quest for single babes. So he would mix up a pitcher of cocktails out in the lot and work on his buzz until he was feeling sufficiently mellow. Then when the time was right he would go into the lounge and mingle amongst the more "loosey-goosey" members of the Sun City female population in hopes of getting lucky.

I have had a number of people say to me that the math skills of high school graduates don't possess the math skills of previous generations. I often wonder if that isn't true. Many years ago when I was in high school my buddy Tom Krispinsky and I went to work in a McDonald's in the Youngstown suburb of Boardman. Before long we were working the cash register at the service window and we had to figure out how much the customer owed by hand. We had to figure out the sales tax and when the customer gave us cash we had to count out the amount of change by hand. We didn't have a button to press that said "hamburger" or "milkshake" and so on. Most of the time the register balanced which is a heck of an accomplishment given the fact that most of us working there were teenagers.

I was at a Circle K convenience store at 16th Street and McDowell and the customer in front of me had purchased $5.00 worth of gas and the clerk was given $10.00. The clerk was fiddling with something down by the floor and she came up and counted out $95.00 in change because the display on the register said that that was how much change was due the customer. Thank goodness the lady in front of me was honest enough to point out the error to the clerk. I thought to myself I had just purchased $5.00 and was about to give her $10.00

as well, I wondered if she had given me more than ninety bucks in change would I be as honest.

A similar case happened one night in Wickenburg, a town northwest of Phoenix on the way to Las Vegas. We all drove up there together and the game ran long. We all figured by the time we got back to town all the bars and restaurants would be closed so we all decided to pick up some beer and munchies and consume them at my house where we all decided to meet that time since I was living in Glendale back then.

We left the high school and right there on the main drag in town there was a drive-thru so we thought that was as good as any place. When it comes to post-game libations we have diverse tastes. So we ended up picking up one twelve pack of Miller Genuine Draft, one twelve pack of Miller Light, a two liter bottle of Coca Cola, a bottle of Arizona Iced Tea, a bag of potato chips, a bag of pork cracklin's and some beef jerky. I gave the gal at the drive-thru window a twenty and hoped it would be enough. I couldn't hear how much it came to but she gave me change and I stuffed it in my shirt pocket without counting it.

We got back to town and were sitting around my back yard when the crew asked me how much all the beer and munchies cost as we were about to settle up with respect to who owed what. I told them I couldn't hear how much it came to but I gave the gal a twenty so let me just count how much change she gave me and we could quickly figure out the tab. I reached into my shirt and counted out the change I had stuffed in there and it came to $18.40 which means she charged us a grand total of one dollar and sixty cents. Every one owed me about forty cents.

After having filled ourselves with beer, soda and pizza or whatever food choice of the night, we usually adjourn to the parking lot for our post-game cigar and to make plans for next week. That is of course if there is a next week. Sooner or later (more often than not sooner) the season comes to an end. It never ceases to amaze me how once the season gets started in the heat of late August or September how quickly you fast forward to late November or December and you are putting the lid on another season.

It seems that for the last ten years or so Roger and I keep saying we're going to retire. At the end of each season the rest of the crew will ask if we intend to come back for another season and each year it is the same response. Roger will say, "If Kovac comes back so will I. I don't want to go out and get with another crew."

At which point I usually will say, "If Roger goes so do I." At the end of each season that is how it goes. A couple years ago the both of us said that season was absolutely going to be it and the last game we were scheduled to officiate was a game at North High.

We were fully prepared to call it a career after that game. That game was one of the worst I had ever been a part of. Neither team really wanted to play since each one had only won a few games. Nobody was in the stands. Each team had a couple of smartass kids we were keeping an eye on. In the second half we threw a bunch of unsportsmanlike conduct flags. Both teams just kind of leaned on each other all night long as opposed to blocking and tackling like they were supposed to. When the final gun sounded, mercifully putting an end to the sloppiest of contests we gladly made our way from the field to the dressing room.

After the game we all went to the Wineburger for a burger and a beer. For the first time in years the topic of whether Roger and I would return was put to rest right away. The other guys asked about next year and I said, "There is no way I'm going to end my career on such a sloppy game," and with that we enjoyed our usual post-game merriment and began making plans for the next season.

CHAPTER XI

9/11

If there was ever a time that sporting events were placed in perspective it was following the terrorist attacks of September 11, 2001.

The morning of the attacks I was in the Emergency Room of the hospital where I was employed at the time dealing with a drunken patient whom we kept tossing out of the ER but kept returning. Someone came in and said that a plane had hit the World Trade Center. I remembered when I was in grade school reading about a plane that struck the Empire State Building causing little damage and at the time I thought that was the case.

In a hospital Emergency Room there are TVs all over the place and this one was no exception. The next thing I know they were showing a second plane hitting the second tower and I knew this was no accident. We resolved the problem with the drunk and not long after that my night shift was over so went home and switched on the TV.

I watched what every other American watched that morning. I saw the World Trade Center collapse, the Pentagon burn, the crash site in Pennsylvania along with the endless commentary. I had a feeling of being kicked in the gut, the likes of which I don't think I've had since I was a kid and came home from school to learn that President Kennedy had been assassinated, only then I think I was too young to fully understand the impact of the event. I couldn't help but wonder if this is how my parents felt on December 7, 1941 when Pearl Harbor was attacked.

It was shortly afterward that one by one all the major sports began canceling contests. Major League Baseball and National Football League games were cancelled and pretty soon college football games of all levels were cancelled as well. It would not have surprised me a bit if our state association cancelled the high school games scheduled for the coming weekend. As the week progressed I kept checking with my fellow crew members and the association but no one had heard anything one way or the other. Late Thursday I learned that the games would go on as scheduled so I made plans to get ready as I usually did.

Our game was scheduled to be played at Shadow Mountain High in northeast Phoenix, a thirty- to forty-five-minute drive from my house via the freeway. At the time we had a Commissioner of Officials who came up with the bright idea that each crew had to submit a video tape of their performance to even be considered for a playoff game that season. Prior to 9/11 I had already made arrangements with the AD at Shadow Mountain to get two field passes for two of my friends who wanted to video tape the game.

Greg Earhart had a video camera and my other buddy Tom McVady had his four- or five-year-old grandson Little Ricky who was already an avid football fan. If you are at Tom's house to watch a football game, Little Ricky positions himself in front of the TV screen and mirrors the referee's hand signals whenever there is a penalty. He even has about a half dozen of them committed to memory. I invited Tom to bring the little guy out to the game and let him down on the sidelines. I figured it would be a heck of an experience for him to be down on the field with "the big guys."

On the day of the game I loaded my equipment bag into my car along with my jug of Gatorade and protein snack and began my trip to Shadow Mountain just like I had done so many Fridays in the past. But this trip would be different. As I drove through the residential neighborhood behind my house en route to the freeway I couldn't help but notice that just about every house had an American flag on display in their yard (working the night shift you kind of miss that sort of stuff). On every other corner there were vendors selling American flags and patriotic T-shirts.

During the week the radio disc jockeys were asking listeners to switch on their headlights during the day as a demonstration of patriotism and solidarity. Well, the message must have gotten out all right since while I drove north on the 101 freeway the southbound rush hour traffic was one long endless ribbon of headlights.

So tremendous was the demand for American flags that some of the local stores that sell them had exhausted their supply. The local newspaper had printed a full page version of the flag for patrons to cut out and tape in their windows.

I arrived at the school at about 5:30 p.m. and to my surprise found the guy with the key right off the bat who also turned out to be the guy with the checks, too. Since I was the first to arrive I was escorted to the dressing room under the home team's grandstands. While doing so I could sense the usual sights and sounds associated with a Friday night high school football game. I could hear the marching band tuning their instruments and saw the majorettes practicing their baton twirling. I could smell hamburgers and hot dogs grilling near the concession stands and heard boosters hawking raffle tickets for the game ball or 50-50 drawings. What seemed to be missing was the pre-game chatter that one associates with a high school sporting event. It was as if the folks there were just sort of going through the motions and that their hearts weren't really in it. At that moment I have to admit I felt the same.

It was not long before the rest of the crew began to arrive and the talk switched to the upcoming contest and things did start to liven up a bit. We dressed and took the field about thirty minutes before the kickoff. My friends were already down on the field along with Little Ricky who called me "Mister Koback." Greg was setting up his video camera and tri-pod on the sideline near the south end zone. I went over to chat with them for a few minutes and then went about my pre-game duties. I still could tell their was an eerie silence but as I got absorbed in my pre-game responsibilities I paid less and less attention to it.

During the opening ceremony the school assembled a group of students in the south end zone with lit candles and there was a moment of silence for those who perished in the terrorist attacks just prior to the National Anthem. I noticed during the National Anthem that just about everyone was singing and singing loudly.

The game began and now there were twenty-two players to keep after and it was going to be a chore because early on it was obvious that the visiting Carl Hayden team was in for a one-sided contest. Just the type of game that can get out of hand in a hurry if you are not careful so an official has to be on his toes as the team that is getting shellacked can easily get frustrated and that is when cheap shots and fights break out. Fortunately on this night both teams behaved admirably. The Shadow Mountain coaching staff scaled back their offense to running plays, nothing fancy. They put in their reserves through the most of the second half. The Carl Hayden kids played clean and demonstrated good sportsmanship all along. The game moved along and we were done in less than two hours.

After the game we showered and went to Uncle Sam's, a pizza joint across from Shadow Mountain High. Afterward, during the drive home I felt a lot better and realized that the game took my mind off the events of the week. I couldn't help but think that maybe the game did the same for those who attended the game as well as for the participants. High school sports in the overall scheme of things isn't the most important thing in the world but on this night was a pleasant departure from the numbing effects of the previous three or four days. It was apparent that despite the events of 9/11 the world was not coming to an end but that it was surely a different one than it was on 9/10.

CHAPTER XII

WRAPPING THINGS UP

Eventually, your season comes to a close and for a lot of officials they send the uniform out to be cleaned and then put it away until next year. They say goodbye to their crew mates and don't see them again until the kickoff meeting the next year. For us that is not nearly the case.

In the years that Ohio State plays at Michigan we try to make it to Ann Arbor, as I said earlier, Roger's brother Fred has season tickets so that is never a problem as it would be if we wanted to go to Columbus.

In yet another of those excursions Roger and I went there and my flight got in really early and that year the temperature was in the sixties, clearly not typical of late November in Michigan. I rode into Detroit to get some pictures of old Tiger Stadium because they closed it down and I figured they would put the wrecking ball to the old ballpark before long. After doing that I returned to the Sheraton out in Romulus, Michigan, where I had rented a room and was just waiting to pick up Roger at the airport, literally, across the street. It was only around five o'clock and I stopped at the hotel bar for some wings and a few beers since his flight was not due until after eleven and I figured to get a few hours' nap in between.

I was at the bar and this guy about thirty-five years old sat down near me and started making small talk. Of course he asked if I was there for the Big Game and I told him I was, and he asked me where I was from and I told him from Arizona, but originally from Youngstown, Ohio. He knew the guy who was just hired as the YSU basketball coach and the guy introduced himself and I told him my first name. He asked if I was going to root for Ohio State and I told him I did not think so. He whined, "Larry from Youngstown, how could you not like Ohio State?" For the umpteenth time I explained to him how when I was growing up college football was not available as it is now on TV and if we wanted to see college football there was the hometown Penguins or if we wanted to take an hour drive to see Kent State or Pittsburg. I also pointed out to him that more than just a few former Youngstown State stand-outs went on to play pro ball like Frank Horvath in the CFL, Craig Cotton of the Detroit Lions and there was this one obscure quarterback that did something no Ohio State QB ever did and that was take his team to the Super Bowl and become one of the game's prominent analysts. I thought he might have heard of him, Ron Jaworski.

After making my point he said, "I suppose you don't like Woody Hayes?" I told him that I wasn't too enamored with some of the old coach's shenanigans like tearing up sideline markers, slugging opposing players and the rest. Again came the whine, "Larry from Youngstown, Ohio, I can't believe you don't like Woody Hayes." So he downed another drink and asked, "I suppose you don't like the Ohio State marching band?"

I was really having fun at this guy's expense as was the bartender, so I said to him, "You know, now that you mention it, that 'Script Ohio' stuff is getting kind of old, don't you think?"

Incredulous, he wailed, "Larry from Youngstown, Ohio, I can't believe you don't like the Ohio State marching band."

I went to lie down for a few hours and then went to pick up Roger at the airport and now it was raining cats and dogs and they were predicting rain for most the game the next day. We stopped real quick at a K-mart nearby and I got a ball cap (a University of Michigan hat that they were literally giving away by the checkout) and a can of spray water repellant since I didn't have a cap that would stand up to an all-day rain. Well we got to the hotel and Roger wanted a bite to eat and I told him the hotel had real good wings in the bar and he said that and a cold beer would be just fine. So we walked into the bar and the guy from earlier was still there with a couple of his buddies that drove up from Columbus. He took one look at Roger and me and then spotted the cap I just bought with its shiny yellow "M" blazing under the bar lights. He yelled out, "Larry from Youngstown, Ohio, I can't believe you're wearing a Michigan hat."

Roger looked at me and asked, "Kovac, is that a friend of yours?" I explained about the earlier conversation and we sat down at the other end of the bar and got our order. So this guy and his buddy asked across the bar if this was my friend that went to Michigan and I told him it was.

Pretty soon, one of his buddies tried to be a smartass and said to Roger, "You know, I don't like you guys from Michigan, never have, never will."

Not to be baited, Roger munched away on his wings and said very matter-of-factly, "Well, that's the way it should be," and he went back to his wings. Obviously, this guy was drunk.

A few minutes later he felt his liquid muscle flexing and said, "I think we're going to kick Michigan's ass."

Undaunted, Roger just responded, "That's just the way you should feel." Now not only was this guy drunk but he was getting frustrated at his own inability to try to piss Roger off.

After a short while we finish and got a couple more beers to take up to our room and as were leaving the guy couldn't resist one parting barb and he said to us, "I can't wait for the game tomorrow and you'll see whose the better team is."

Roger and I just walked out and he bade him a farewell with one final reply, "I wouldn't have it any other way." The following morning we got up early to head to Ann Arbor and meet up with Kenny and Fred and to get something to eat before the game. As we were leaving our room there was the loudmouth hurling into a planter near the elevator and I couldn't help later thinking after Michigan once again beat Ohio State that how hung over the guy had to have been along with the long drive back to Columbus and another Big Game defeat.

    First and foremost with the arrival of the holidays comes the annual Thanksgiving Feast at the McVady household, something that began for me back in about oh, 1988 or so. I was working with Tom at the hospital and as usual I had just broken up with yet another girlfriend. My close friends to this day maintain steadfastly that I do this purposely to avoid having to buy them Christmas presents but it just seems to work out that way. I don't know if they originally felt sorry for me since I didn't have family in the area and all my friends had families of their own, but they invited me over one year and I began going there every year if for any other reason to provide entertainment for his kids' enjoyment. Of course it was never planned that way, it just seemed to happen that way. It is not as if we did not use Tom's kids for assisting us older folks in our own indulgences. After beer prices at Spring Training games sky-rocketed in the late 1980s and Game Staff posted at the entrances to assure that no libations were smuggled into the games, what better way to sneak a few brews past the ever vigilant than to enlist his two daughters as assistants in that endeavor? While the folks at the gates were ardently screening the adults for contraband, Tom's eight- and ten-year-old daughters, Katie and Jennifer, were cheerfully entering the ballpark with a few beers tucked away neatly in their sleeping bags.

    Well, anyway, if some of the more light-hearted moments at Thanksgiving brought a little mirth to them well, the trade off was more than fair. Like the one year Gracie, one of the two McVady pooches, a nearly blind and gimpy, collie-like dog used me as an after dinner snack. For some reason that dog did not care for me and used to growl at me as soon as I walked through the door, but because of Gracie's ills she posed little threat to anyone's safety, that is except for the one year she mustered up enough strength to leap up and bite me right on the ass, precisely where the handkerchief pocket was on my jeans. That dog even broke the skin, the weird part was after she did that she was always friendly to me thereafter all the way up until she had to be put down a couple years ago.

The very next time I went to Tom's house I sat down and Gracie started over toward me and usually when I showed up one of his kids would get the leash and hook him to the kitchen table. But before anyone could do so she came up to me and put her head on my leg and wanted me to pet her. I just figured her eyesight was getting worse. Another year his grandson Little Ricky got into the act. He couldn't have been more than a year or and was just starting to walk. He walked up to me while I was sitting on the couch and we were having a good old time until he pissed all over me. I made a habit of not wearing good clothes over to Tom's.

The Annual Pierogi Press Off is usually a week or two before Christmas. This is a tradition begun by me and my friend Tom McVady back in the 1980s. Tom and I were working together at the hospital and we were discussing ethnic foods and Tom's wife Jo is Polish and me being Slovak are big fans of the food Pierogis. We were saying that you could not get good pierogis in Arizona (actually there is a lot of stuff that you can't that is any good, like pizza). This is dough that is rolled flat and cut into about three inch circles which are then stuffed with mashed potatoes, mushroom or sauerkraut. Half the circle is then folded over the stuffing and the ends pressed together kind of like a ravioli and then tossed into a pot of boiling water. When they rise to the surface they are fully cooked. At that point we usually toss them into the freezer and into plastic zipper bags to be cooked a few at a time.

I have invited the guys from the crew over from time to time and we usually sit around pressing pierogis and drinking beer, lots of beer. Since the process requires rolling them in flour so they don't stick to the rolling surface, considerable amounts of flour end up on the floor, on the carpet, on the counter, on the stove and generally just about everywhere. I used to have a housekeeper that came in every several weeks and during the Pierogi Press Off time of year I used to pay her extra. In recent years we started to make our own Polish sausage from scratch. I mean grinding the pork and mixing in the spices and stuffing the hog casings like my mom and dad used to do with our neighbor Mrs. Zibrik back in Youngstown. The last year in Arizona before I got disabled we outdid ourselves when we made 156 pierogis and ten pounds of Polish sausage. The house had so much flour strewn around it added to the holiday festivities kind of like a fresh dusting of snow.

My housekeeper quit that year.

Now allow me to explain here that I have not always been a good cook and for the longest time all I could do was cook hamburgers, having only acquired that skill in my days at McDonald's just out of high school. In the years I was a policeman my first wife and I used to work opposite shifts so when I got home at eleven or twelve o'clock at night, or whenever, all I got was cold leftovers. So gradually I began to learn how to cook different stuff over the years, more as a necessity and eventually learned to enjoy it, especially when I would whip up something really good and see my friends enjoying it.

In the years after I got divorced it was a real asset to have when meeting women and hell, if you can get them to come over to your place for you to cook for them half the battle is won.

Following the Pierogi Press Off is the New Year's Day Feast where I invite all my friends over for food and football. It's my sort of mass Christmas present to them all.

Over the years I have become one who does not over-indulge on New Year's Eve when all lot of folks who don't drink 364 days a year try to make up for it in one night. That is partly the reason that I am able to start cooking at about two o'clock in the morning on New Year's Day which is when I get up and prepare the trademark "Apples and Sausage Stuffing*" that I use to stuff the turkey that is just one of the dishes that I prepare for the New Year's Day Feast. The recipe was given to me many years ago by an old Jewish lady and it so good that often I make a separate batch because my guests like to take some home with them.

Just prior to going to bed the night before, I take navy beans and soak them overnight. I'll tell you why soon enough.

Once the turkey is in the oven I get out the pork spare ribs and throw them under the broiler for about ten minutes, or if I have already put the turkey in I throw them on the gas grill on high for the ten minutes. Once they are rinsed off I put them in the crock pot with sauerkraut to cook for six to eight hours. This is a tradition dating back to when I was a kid. I don't know the reason but my mother used to makes ribs and sauerkraut every New Year's Day. I know that the Mexicans have "Menudo," a soup-like dish with Tripe. They tell me that the tripe, which is stomach, absorbs the alcohol from the night before. All I can think of is, at least in my case sauerkraut goes through the system so rapidly that it flushes out everything from the night before. So maybe that is how it became a Slovak tradition on New Year's Day. Nonetheless it gets consumed quickly so if you want some get to my house early.

For Christmas I usually get a store-bought spiral cut ham for Christmas dinner and I save the bone. I take the beans out of the fridge and sit the bone down in that and cook it with some garlic and onions for ham and beans. One of the guys I work with likes to come over for just the ham and beans. He likes to take the part that sticks to the bottom of the pot especially and he is more than welcome to take some with him to work.

I usually time it so that everything is done at just about noon and the guys start to trickle in about then. Tom comes over and brings with him deviled eggs.

I think you can see where this is headed. If you can't, here it is. I never planned it this way but all the goodies consumed at the New Year's Day Feast along with the malted beverages have a tendency to cause a flatulent reaction even in the healthiest of constitutions and that usually kicks in about the time my guests return home to their respective spouses or girlfriends who at one time or another have called this to my attention.

Less than a month later comes Super Bowl Sunday and I make a batch of chili and if it doesn't rain I will go out on the grill and make ribs. Growing up in Youngstown, Ohio, there was a black man who was a friend of the family, "Shorty" Underwood. Shortly lived out on what was called the Sharon Line in part of the city that was once serviced by a street car line that old-timers say ran from Youngstown through Hubbard, Ohio, terminating in nearby Sharon, Pennsylvania. With the invention of the automobile, the streetcar outlived its usefulness and the streetcar tracks were paved over on what is now Jacobs Road. Shorty had a one-bedroom house off of Jacobs Road and in the summer time would have picnics that would attract dozens, at which time he would make ribs that had a sauce that I have never seen duplicated. These were the best ribs I ever tasted, but the sauce was the secret. You would go to his house and pick up the ribs and his wife Dorothy would ask if you wanted sauce and you would have to be a fool to say no, and she would have you follow her into the house and the kitchen where she would open the oven and there would be a roasting pan full of mason jars full of the sauce that was a cross between red and dark orange. She would take out a jar which was too hot to hold in your hand and put in a bag. When you got the sauce home and opened it there was always a half of a lemon floating on top. There was never any sauce on the ribs as you would have to add it on your own.

    While waiting for the sauce to cool Shorty knew that I was a catcher on a fast pitch softball team and he would go somewhere back in that small house of his and retrieve an old mitt and softball and we would go alongside of his house and he would display his skills as a fast pitch pitcher. I mean to tell you this guy could have pitched for any team I played for or against. His favorite trick was where he had two trees about fifty feet apart in his side yard and he would stand to one side of one of the trees and I would take a position on the opposite side of the furthest tree and he would uncork a mind-boggling pitch that would begin to the left of the tree he was standing next to and curve to the right of the tree I was standing on the opposite side of. When he would do this it would attract onlookers from among the picnic goers at his house and this would result in claps and whistles from the crowd.

In the early 1970s Shorty died at the young age of forty-four and within six months his wife Dorothy died, also. His only son I heard died in California and the secret of his sauce went with him to the grave.

Well, wouldn't you know it, Tom McVady and I were at work and saying how you could not get good ribs in Arizona and the subject of Shorty's sauce came up. Tom had worked at America West Airlines for a while and he was telling me that he had a co-worker whom he referred to only as "Mr. Shy."

"Mr. Shy" too, was black and prided himself on his ribs which apparently, he too, did not use sauce in the cooking process but added afterward or at least in the final stage. Whoever "Mr. Shy" was, by the time Tom and I were discussing him he was in jail for some heinous offense, but not like Shorty had given him the ingredients for his sauce before getting locked up and Tom gave it to me.

I have tried it and it is the closest thing to Shorty Underwood's sauce I have ever tasted, but instead of lemon you use grapefruit in "Mr. Shy's Barbecue Sauce*" that can be made with simple items you get in any grocery store like ketchup, molasses and steak sauce, etc.

The off-season is a time that some officials who are disgruntled with their present crew begin an off-season political campaign in an effort to find another crew or get bigger and better games. Like I have said the guys I work with are like friends and I wouldn't dream of trying to hook up with anybody else or lobby for better games. I know when the schedule comes out all the games I will get are on the far west side, as far from home as they can send me. One year Roger went to France with his wife and when he returned he had a box of French chocolates and gave them to the gal that made out the schedules for football. Well, hell, wouldn't you know it we got a worse schedule than the previous season. So much for French chocolates.

A few years back a lot of officials were griping that the same crews got all the big games and the Commissioner at the time flatly denied that he played favorites and his Chief Observer, the hefty

Casper Crew Commish stood steadfastly behind the Commissioner's assertions. That myth got exploded all to hell when one official was at a high school baseball game and ran into one of the football crew chiefs who was also a baseball umpire. This particular crew chief was just one of those supposed "elite" crew chiefs and was telling this other official that he was "guaranteed" a State Football Championship game, it was just a question whether it was a 4-A or 5-A game that he was going to do. Well, in Arizona the 4-A and 5-A Championship football game is always televised and sure as Christ made green apples, there was "Elephant Ass" with his crew working one of the games. I was more than a little pissed at this as there were a lot of other officials who thought what is the good of attending off-season clinics and impressing the Observers and all the other stuff that they tell you will improve your chance of getting a playoff game when the deck is stacked against you and your crew three months before the season even starts.

A few years back as usual our season had come to a close but there were three weeks left in the season and I was asked to substitute on another two other crews at three big games that were scheduled. What our association does is send out the schedule for the first seven weeks of the season and then the last three weeks they try to schedule the stronger crews for the games that have playoff implications. It was three of those such games that I got the opportunity to work. In fact, they were good games. Afterward, I met up with Roger and the guys at a Pop Warner game we were doing and I told them that although they were the big time games, those elite crew did not do anything any different than we did and there were some things that I thought we did better. Of course, that was one of the years that I went back to Ohio for a visit in November figuring the season would be over and wouldn't you know we got a playoff game. It was after I returned when I found out that the head of the Casper Crew himself came out to personally evaluate our crew and after the game he had such helpful comments like, "The problem is some officials don't know when it is time to hang it up." According to Scott, he was looking right at Roger when he said that. Evidently, he has never forgiven Roger and me for exposing his phony credentials when he crowed about being a Big Ten official years ago. Some people have such thin skin.

I think some crews are a little jealous when they see our crew and how we keep together during the off-season and it was after one of those seasons that the Commissioner at the time gave me a call and tried to get me to jump crews. He said that I "was going nowhere with those guys and you ought to be on one of the more 'elite' crews." Of course he would be just delighted to assist me in any such quest and all I had to do was give the word and he would make a few calls. I told him that I was perfectly happy where I was at and basically thanks, but no thanks.

The off-season is a good time to effect change and that is the job of the Board and after one season in the late 1980s Roger and I both ran for the Board and were elected in our respective regions.

The Board consisted of a dozen or so representatives from different geographic regions around the area and there are different committees. There are guidelines set for the training of new officials and the continuing education of current officials. A real effort is made to help move the newer officials up the ladder that are deserving of it. Once the season starts they collect ratings from coaches and the Board's recommendations for playoff crews is supposed to be considered by the Commissioner. The Board members put a lot of time into the organization and do not get a penny for their service. I had the good fortune of serving on the Evaluations and Ratings Committee that works with the newer officials and helps them get the assistance they need to progress sufficiently and also helps them by showing them how to document that progress. We would sit down with the new officials and explain to them how to approach an older official that they may work with at a frosh, JV or Pop Warner game and hand them a short form we provided for them to have the older official fill out. The key is getting as many favorable evaluations that they can. At the time if you were a newer official, a level 3, 4 or 5 you could get an evaluation from any Certified or Level 1 official. At a Pop Warner game they may work with more than one

Level 1 official in one game and the secret was to get an evaluation (preferably a favorable one) from each of them.

If the official worked two games with two or more Level 1 officials, he could conceivably get four to six evaluations in one day. At season's end we stressed that it was the official's responsibility that this information gets back to the Board, not another Board member. This was because a number of newer officials turned their ratings sheets over to one Board member who promised them he would bring the data to the Board meeting that would be held annually to determine which officials were to be moved up that year. At the last minute the Board member in question dropped the ball and never made it to the move-up meeting and some deserving officials did not get their case argued before the Board or their evaluations brought up for discussion. As members of the Evaluations Committee we tried to stress to the newer officials that it was their responsibility to make sure that all the positive info regarding their performance be brought as out into the open as possible. The more exposure they got to more experienced officials the better their chances of being moved up.

I was a little surprised at the several officials who served on the Board for purposes of their own agenda and some of the sniping that went on at Board meetings made me wonder if some of these guys thought that they were serving on the Board of Directors for a Fortune 500 company rather than just high school football. But, for the most part though, the group had good intentions. Part of the Board was the Mechanics Committee who were the guys that put on the Mechanics Clinics each year. As I surmised early on, the Mechanics Committee devoted a lot of time and effort into their endeavors and I was glad I paid attention in those early years to what they had to say to the new officials. They were the hardest working committee and it showed. If you are a new official, it cannot be stressed that if you are going to make the correct call in a play you have to be in the proper position to see what is actually happening. A line judge cannot accurately locate the spot to place the ball for the next play if he is ten yards behind the play and the Mechanics

Committee works to accomplish that goal. They don't tell what the proper call is so much as where each position on the crew should be during any specific play and that is the key to good officiating. You can call what you see, if you are there to see it and as I mentioned early on, "sell the call."

After seeing the effort those committee members put into those clinics leads me to give aspiring officials a bit of advise. If your state or local association has such a committee, and I'm sure that it does, when they hold these clinics for you, if for anything other than respect, shut up and pay attention. Don't act like you're in tenth grade study hall and talk back and forth when you should be paying attention, because if those guys put forth half of the effort of the guys I knew, they know the mechanics backwards and forwards, this stuff is for you. You won't have a good time officiating if you're constantly out of position because you'll have the coaches, players, fans and other officials on your ass so bad you'll want to hide under the grandstands.

Of course being friends during the off-season it only stands to reason that between Spring Training baseball games and trips to Laughlin to gamble(strictly small time) there is the occasional favor. Even those provide some of life's more daft moments. One such moment occurred one spring afternoon when I had a day off during the week. Roger at the time was seeing this gal who was a flight attendant for one of the major air carriers that flew out of Sky Harbor Airport.

For the last twenty-five years or so I have always driven a pickup truck or truck of some sort, like now it's a Blazer. Being over six feet tall they are easier to get in and out of than a passenger car and I am always hauling stuff around, not to mention the free libations around the holidays after helping one buddy or another get his Christmas tree.

Well, this gal Roger knew had her eye on a king size mattress and box spring set at a local furniture store that was going out of business and was selling some name brand bedding at a fraction of the cost, but you had to pick it up yourself because they had either sold off all their delivery trucks or had them seized by the court or whatever. Anyhow Roger called me and said if I helped him pick up and deliver this monstrosity the lady would fill my tank with gas, give me a six pack of Heineken and ten bucks for my trouble. All of which would require about an hour of my time. Quite a quick payday for such little effort. The mattress was outside the store and had guys to load it on the truck and she had a new, big house with the master bedroom on the first floor (no steps) right off the front door, so I thought, what the heck!

When we get to the store, Roger brought ONE elastic bungee strap to tie the mattress down. The box spring came in two pieces, but fit nicely into the bed of the truck but the mattress hung over the sides slightly. Still, it had enough heft that I felt sure that it would not budge. Besides, we stayed off the main roads where I didn't crank it up and kept the speed under thirty-five miles per hour. The store was in central Phoenix at Central and Camelback and she lived in east Scottsdale, a distance of about fifteen miles. At about a mile and a half from her house we stopped at a huge gas station, "The Super Pumper," for my free tankful and so far everything looked tight. We headed back on to Shea Boulevard for the remaining trip to her house and Roger drove on to make sure she had everything ready.

Traffic on Shea Boulevard is posted at about forty-five miles per hour but nobody goes less than sixty. I kept my speed conservative and just before the turn off to her street I pulled over into the left turn lane and began to slow down when in the other direction a huge Mayflower moving van (imagine the irony) whizzed by going eastbound at what seemed like seventy miles an hour and the wind blast kicked up in its wake felt like a small tornado. In the rear view mirror I saw the pale blue mattress somersaulting end over end across three lanes of traffic until getting run over by a cable TV installer's pick up truck that was east bound behind me. I stopped, got out and ran back only to find that the mattress was wedged between the left front tire and the wheel well and if that was not bad enough there was smoke billowing out from underneath it because the friction from being dragged several hundred yards over the hot blacktop had set the damn thing on fire.

Many years ago I had an old sergeant on Youngstown Police say that Youngstown was such a violent town that there had to be a guardian angel of sorts looking after us because there were so few of us that had been shot or killed. I am becoming a believer because that guardian angel has had a way of showing up from time to time in some of my life's more precarious moments.

So there I was, me and the cable guy with the mattress lodged under his truck and the only others in sight were an old guy about eighty walking down the sidewalk with his wife hooked up to an oxygen tank on wheels. He came up to us and out of the clear blue sky said, "I used to be in the delivery business and know just what to do!" He pointed to a spot where the top of the mattress was arched in the middle from being stuck under the wheels and said, "Put all your weight on there!" Then he told the driver to get back in the truck and gently putting it in gear and alternately rock it back and forth from "drive" to "reverse" and back again until the mattress was dislodged. "But," he warned, "be careful because if there is one slip, you (meaning me) could get dragged under the wheels." Reluctantly, the driver got back in and began to alternately move the truck back and forth and before long the mattress got dislodged.

By this time Roger figured something must have happened and doubled back just as we were stomping out the smoldering mattress. One side of it looked okay except for a tire mark or two but the other side had a scorched hole in the fabric about six to eight inches in diameter and was still smoking. He said, "Well, let's press on!" and helped me load it back on the truck and we went the final two or three blocks to the stewardess's house.

When we got there we carried in the box springs first and then the mattress last. I guess Roger, like myself, grew up watching re-runs of *Laurel and Hardy* or *The Three Stooges* and we carried the mattress with the good side facing the side of the doorway where the lady was standing holding the door opened, with the scorched side facing away from her so she couldn't see it, and we almost pulled it off, if it weren't for her damned dog that smelled the smoke (it began smoldering again) and began barking to beat the band. She came around to the other side and took one look at it and her jaw dropped and all she could gasp was, "My mattress."

To which Roger responded, "Ah, it ain't that bad, besides you know how good you are, a little needle and thread and you won't be able to tell the difference!" We carried it into the bedroom and leaned it against the wall while she put out the smoldering with a wet washcloth. I felt bad enough and he said, "Well, give Kovac the beer and the ten bucks like you promised." I figured she was going to call her lawyer when she left the room and she came back with the six pack and handed me ten dollars out of her wallet. I high tailed it the hell out of there and left the two of them in the living room. I talked with Roger that weekend and he assured me that she did not throw the mattress out and that other than the slight smoky aroma that lingered she was using the mattress and with the proper sheets and covers you couldn't really tell what the history the mattress carried with it during its young life.

The off-season is a time when you may gauge your performance or experiences on the field with previous years and decide that sooner or later your career is coming to an end. In my case the decision was taken out of my hands when in 2003, inexplicably I awoke one morning to find out there was no strength in my legs. Originally, since I was sick to my stomach I attributed it to a severe case of the flu but when I began to feel better and could not regain the strength in my legs it was clear that there was something seriously wrong.

I went to the doctor and they poked and prodded and took one blood test after another but nothing seemed to help. I found myself falling down for no reason and was very unsteady on my feet to the point I was using a wheelchair and a walker. It wasn't until I went to a neurologist who had an MRI performed that they diagnosed the problem as two bulging discs that were putting pressure on some nerve that goes into my legs and thus the lack of strength. I was put on a regimen of physical therapy and not long afterward I retired. Since all my life I have had to physically struggle with combative people and lift heavy objects (i.e. dead bodies, fire extinguishers, etc.) it was clear that I could not continue in that capacity.

Only now can I appreciate the plight of the aged and handicapped because there were lots of times I needed to use those blue placards they give you for the handicapped parking and ramps instead of steps.

In October of 2003 I sold my house and returned to football-rich northeast Ohio and the thought of ever officiating another high school football game was merely a dream. Upon my return to Ohio I have married my new wife Jacqueline also from northeast Ohio, Madison to be exact.

I keep in touch with my old crew members and of course my friend Tom Krispinsky. I kept up my physical rehab but at first was doing it only half-heartedly. But once again high school football figured into the equation. We have settled in to a small town in the northeast corner of the state, primarily Conneaut, Ohio. I bought an exercise bike and slowly have been able to throw away the walker and progressed to where I can walk with the use of a cane. Last year I got a wild hair up my ass, as my dad used to say, and drove up to the local high school stadium a few blocks from my house. I parked along a side street and watched the beginning of a game on a Friday night in October. The local team did not have too successful a season but the town turned out in big numbers for the game. I saw the five officials standing along the sideline before the game and felt a lump swelling up in my throat and my eyes watering. Before long I couldn't watch any more and I found that I didn't last through the first quarter.

Since then I haven't taken my physical rehab so half-heartedly and I am using the goal of one day returning to field once again. As I told my friend Tom Krispinsky, if I approach it like the upcoming season is the one in which I make my return to the officiating field I will be motivated to work harder. That way, even if I fall short of my goal of returning to the field at least I will have taken steps to increase my physical well-being and to keep active, which in itself is good for me in the long run.

Maybe I won't be putting on the old black and white striped shirt this season but the motivation has allowed me to get rid of the cane and the walker entirely to walk on my own and this past Christmas I was even able to go to the mall and buy my wife's present for the first time in three years. Like Ron Demesko tells my brother when he gets on his case to lose weight since he is diabetic, it is going to take focus and dedication to accomplish that goal, and I think he is right to the point. Ron is in his sixties and looks like he could still play semi-pro football like he once did for the Norfolk Neptunes.

Recently, I watched a tape of a local high school football telecast and the referee was a guy that moved and looked like old Elmer, my old crew chief. Dennis McCabe says that they are crying for good officials in this area and at fifty-four maybe that day for me is once again in my future, hopefully sooner than later. I recently had an occasion to contact my old association in Arizona in hopes of getting a letter verifying my years of experience there. If the letter is any indication, I guess they held me in higher regard than I thought they did all these years as they had some nice things to say about me. This was done out of hope of one day coming out of retirement, as Ohio recognizes officials with out-of-state experience and I hope that when that day comes that I can only have the good fortune of landing on a great group of guys that do a good job and go out there on Friday nights to have a good time for two and a half hours. I could only hope that there are four or five guys with the same personalities like the guys I was with for oh, twenty years or so. That makes those Friday a hell of a lot of fun because, seriously, it's just high school football!

THE END

APPLE AND SAUSAGE STUFFING
(DOUBLE BATCH)

2½ lbs. of sausage
2 large onions, diced
7 celery stalks, diced
6 to 7 medium apples, cored, peeled and diced
2 12 oz. bags of croutons
3 cans Chicken w/ Rice Soup
1 bag Lipton's Onion & Mushroom Soup Mix

In large pot brown sausage draining any excess grease.

In separate skillet sauté onions, celery and apples in margarine until tender.

Add to sausage in pot, add soup cans and mix and simmer for 20 minutes covered. Remove from heat and season to taste.

Mix in croutons, cover and refrigerate overnight.

Makes enough to stuff a chicken. The San Diego Chicken.

MISTER SHY'S SAUCE

1 32 oz. bottle of catsup
1 8 oz. bottle of A-1 Steak Sauce
3 tablespoons of brown sugar
3 tablespoons of molasses
1 tablespoon of grapefruit juice and ¼ grapefruit rind

Place ingredients in sauce pan and simmer for about fifteen minutes, stirring frequently.
Remove from heat.
Use on barbecued chicken or ribs.
Sauce may be stored for up to two weeks in sealed, refrigerated container.

Printed in the United States
67563LVS00002B/138